THE MOTHER OF US ALL

Divine Mother Speaks

A WAY FORWARD

Channeled and Written by

Robin H. Lysne, Ph.D.

Publication Page

The Mother of Us All - Divine Mother Speaks - A Way Forward

Cover Photograph by G. Brad Lewis, Photographer

Blue Bone Books
P.O. Box 2250
Santa Cruz, CA 95063
United States of America

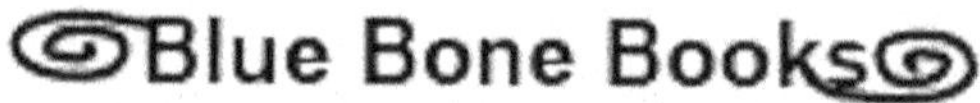

Santa Cruz, CA

ISBN#: 978-1-948675-15-4

Library of Congress#: 2023924312

Ebook: 978-1-948675-16-1

Table of Contents

Publication Page ii
Table of Contents iii
Introduction - The Mother Aspect of God by Tyagi Jayadev - 2
Chapter One - Divine Mother, How to Speak and Listen to Her for Our Future Sustainability and Peace - 9
Chapter Two - Her Helpers and The Sacred Mountain - 14
Chapter Three - Meeting Mo's Family - 22
Chapter Four - Giant Lessons from Big Mo - 25
Chapter Five - Meeting Mother Gaia - 33
Chapter Six - Meeting the Spirit of Mt. Tuyshtak Again - 44
Chapter Seven - Mo Speaks to Me -49
Chapter Eight - Reconnecting to Mother Earth -52
Chapter Nine - Many ways that Divine Mother Speaks through Her Guidance for Us and through Gaia - 55
Chapter Ten - More Messages from Divine Mother: On The Earth, Ocean, and our Interactions - 74
Chapter Eleven - The Soil of the Soul: Your Life Purpose on Mother Gaia - 86
Chapter Twelve - Divine Earth Mother- Forgiveness as Key to Releasing Karma - 96
Chapter Thirteen - Humans and Nature - 101
Chapter Fourteen - Mother Earth Meditation Group: The Power of Prayer - 107
Chapter Fifteen - Divine Mother Speaks about Evolution and Levels of Consciousness - 123
Chapter Sixteen- Stories of Challenges and Friends - 140
Chapter Seventeen - Heart Path helps Us Come Into Star Essence or Our Authentic Nature - 147
Chapter Eighteen - Divine Mother's Vision of The Future - 162
Author Bio - 165

Dedicated to
Mother-Father God
or All-That-Is

The Mother of Us All by Dr. Robin Lysne is a book well worth the attention of the spiritual seeker. In this collection of channeled material, Robin has recorded messages she has received either for herself, others or both.

The quality of what comes through a channel can best be assessed by some of the classic criteria used to assess other spiritual experiences. Those criteria I wish to highlight are: 1. How does it fit with tradition(s) and community? (The traditions and community may often include scripture and other written sources, as well as the teaching of guru and conversation with spiritual friends.) 2. How does it affect your heart?

In her writing Robin makes clear connections with the traditions of which she is a part. That integration is crucial and well-done. But most important for me, as I was reading the book, I found my heart opening. That opening is a very good thing indeed, and is a significant goal and well as means on the spiritual path.

I hope you read this book. And I hope your heart opens as well.

Nirmoha Neil Vargas-Gladen, M.Div.
Lead Chaplain at Hospice of Santa Cruz County
Ananda Lightbearer and Life Sevaka Member
Pilgrim in the Nayaswami order
Articles published in the area of spiritual development and therapy

THE MOTHER OF US ALL

Divine Mother Speaks

A WAY FORWARD

channeled and
written by

Robin H. Lysne, Ph.D.

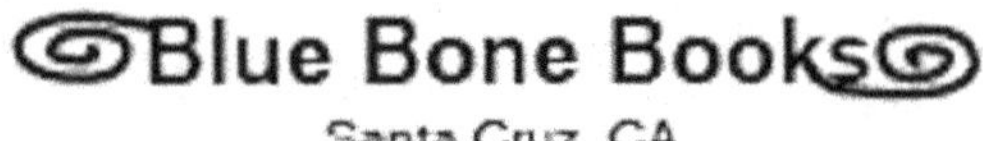

Santa Cruz, CA

left: Paramahansa Yogananda,
right: Amma
Below left: Anandamayi Ma
right: Her Husband, Ramani Mohan Chakrabarti, Anandamayi Ma, and Paramahansa Yogananda.

Divine Mother Speaks
A Way Forward

Introduction

The Mother Aspect of God - by Tyagi Jayadev

For centuries, across the world, there has been an imbalance that favors masculine energy. This is evident in the realms of religion, where God is generally described as "God the Father." Paramhansa Yogananda tried to changc this unilateral approach and used himself as an example.

Paramhansa Yogananda:

I myself worship the Mother aspect [of God] especially. For the Mother is closer than the Father. The Father aspect of God represents that part which is aloof from His creation. The Mother is creation itself. Even among mankind, the human father is more disposed than the mother to judge their erring children. The mother always forgives.

Paramhansa Yogananda explains:

The Divine Mother is so beautiful! But remember, in Her higher manifestation even that beauty is formless. She is in everything. Her divine, compassionate love is expressed in the raindrops. Her beauty is reflected in the colors of the rainbow. She offers fresh hope to mankind with the rose-tinted clouds at dawn. Above all, be ever conscious of Her presence in your heart.

Who is Divine Mother?

She has many names. Some call her Star Woman (darkness behind the Stars from several Native American paths)[1], Kali, Holy Ghost, Mâ Ananda Moyî (Ananda Moi Ma), Mother Meera, Amma, Mother Mary, Black Madonna, Virgin of Guadalupe and many other names.

Mother Earth is known today as Gaia. Each and every woman who nurtures others; every caregiving man with compassion are extentions of Divine Mother. Divine Mother is an energetic reality of beauty, love and compassion that lives around us and inside each of us, and all through nature. Divine Mother assumes countless forms in all of us. Here are some ways we see her in various religions:

Christianity: Mother Mary: The mother of Jesus, who is Divine Mother. Mary Magdalene: Jesus's closest disciple, and some reference her as his wife in the 2nd century early documents. Later in the patriarchal church they called her a prostitute to put her down. As a devotee, Jesus cleared negative demons from her and she was incredibly loyal to him.

Black Madonna: Ancient representation of Mother Mary, and previously from African origin.

Virgin of Guadalupe: Mother Mary appeared to Juan Diego in 1531 and was named Virgin of Guadalupe and holds a special place in Mexican culture and history.

There are over twenty other women saints in the Catholic church,

---

1 Added by Robin Lysne from her connection to the Native American path.

but these are the main ones who knew him, and the Black Madonna was considered Mother Mary.

Hinduism: Kali: Paramhansa Yogananda worshipped the Divine Mother in the form of Kali. In *Autobiography of a Yogi* we read how, as a child, his intense prayers to Her miraculously secured him two desired kites. Years later when he grew up, a Kali statue came to life for him—moving, loving, and speaking to him. He explains:

> *Kali represents Mother Nature. She is AUM, the cosmic vibration. In AUM everything exists–all matter, all energy, and the thoughts of all conscious beings. Hence, Her garland of heads, to show that She is invisibly present in all minds." Her tongue sticks out; she has four arms, all of which are symbols of nature. In an inner vision, She becomes extremely beautiful. After a meditation, Yogananda once exclaimed, "AUM is Divine Mother. AUM Kali! AUM Kali! AUM Kali! Listen: Oh, how beautiful it is! AUM Kali! AUM Kali! AUM Kali!"*

Durga: Yogananda and his guru Sri Yukteswar held "annual festivities of Durgapuja," worshipping Mother Durga. In *Autobiography of a Yogi* Yogananda explains:

> *[Durga] is the Inaccessible, an aspect of Divine Mother, Shakti, the female creative force [AUM] personified.*

Durga is powerful, also known as the slayer of demons, meaning the dark inner enemies of our souls.

Saraswati: Described in *Autobiography of a Yogi* as the "goddess of wisdom," Saraswati "is symbolized as performing on the vina, mother of all stringed instruments." In mythology, She is Brahma's wife and holds a profound symbolism. Readers who want to explore the deep inner meaning of the various Indian goddesses will find enlightening explanations in Swami Kriyananda's book *The Hindu Way of Awakening.*

Lakshmi: Is the much-loved goddess of abundance and prosperity. She is Vishnu's wife. Yogananda says she is the primordial Nature.

Parvati: In the *Autobiography of a Yogi*, Yogananda addresses Sri Yukteswar with these devotional words:

> *"Guruji," I said, "from my twelfth year on, I have made many unsuccessful attempts to reach the Himalayas. I am finally convinced that without your blessings the Goddess Parvati will not receive me!"*

Parvati is literally explained as *Of the mountains.* Parvati, mythologically represented as a daughter of Himavat or the sacred mountains, is a name given to the Shakti, or consort of Shiva.

Chamundi: Yogananda, in his universal spirit, reverently bowed to many forms of Divine Mother. For example, we read in *Autobiography of a Yogi*:

> *There [in Mysore] we had bowed before the gold and silver altars of the Goddess Chamundi, the patron deity of the family of the reigning Maharaja.*

Chamundi, an aspect of Chandi (Parvati), is a lesser-known goddess but nonetheless represents for us one of Divine Mother's countless forms. Who could ever limit Her?

Buddhism: Buddhists revere many goddesses, the most famous being Tara, the Mother of Liberation. Quan Yin is another significant goddess who supports compassion in many Asia cultures. She often has a thousand eyes and hands with compassion and help reaching all beings who cry out.

Judaism: Hebrews have only one God, Yahweh, but the Shechinah is His dwelling within; His presence is a feminine word and quality.

Islam: Muslims similarly worship only one God, Allah. Fatima, the immaculate and venerated daughter of the prophet Mohammed, "The first of the women of Paradise", represents the feminine presence in Islam. Muslims have a rosary-like prayer known as Tasbih Fatima, meaning Fatima's glorification of God.

Spiritual rather than Religious Beliefs added by Robin Lysne: There are many people all over the world that have direct understanding of Mother Nature and cherish that relationship with her. Many of these people are Indigenous people who still maintain a deep and clear relationship with the Earth in their Earth-based traditions. Rather than beliefs they share experiences and give people ways to connect with the Earth Mother, so we can all talk to her and love her as she gives us everything we need.

Her Earthly Face

Divine Mother is extremely close to us in very a tangible way. How? Every woman can become a living Divine Mother here on Earth—an instrument of Her pure love, Her pure grace, and Her pure power. When that happens, it is Her appearance right in front of us. Her love and presence is amazing as she radiates Love for All -There Is in all of us.

Secretly the Divine Mother also wears the face of our earthly mothers (however imperfectly she may play that role). In *Autobiography of a Yogi* it's recorded that She tells Yogananda:

> *It is I who have watched over thee, life after life, in the tenderness of many mothers! See in My gaze the two black eyes, the lost beautiful eyes, thou seekest!*

Yogananda lost his earthly mother, with her beloved "solacing black eyes," at the tender age of eleven. This tragic event pushed him to intensely seek the Cosmic Mother. She finally appeared to him one day, consoling him with words, which apply to all of us, Her children:

> *Always have I loved thee!*
> *Ever shall I love thee!*

We do well to meditate on Her words, again and again, immersing ourselves in Her eternal love.[2]

Listening to Divine Mother Today By Robin Lysne

The first time I experienced Divine Mother was when I needed extra help. In 1998 after losing my only child, I experienced Divine Mother coming to me and speaking to me about what I was to do rather than having children. She said, "You are here to serve many mothers, and many children who will need your help."

After that I started a private practice in energy healing after having a massage therapy practice for almost ten years. It became clear to me that I could continue to help others.

---

2 Most of these last six pages are from an Ananda Website about Yogananda and Divine Mother by Tyagi Jayadev: https://www.ananda.org/blog/the-many-faces-of-divine-mother/

In 2004, I was guided by Divine Mother and WuLan, a master guide and teacher, to begin a group focused on channeling their spirits. I had created four groups that eventually became one larger group. I have been channeling Divine Mother, Star Woman, Angels and Archangels, for those who are open to listening to what they have to say about all of us and what goes on around us. I have been bringing her in to groups of people as Star Woman (Native American name for Star Essence Presence), and Divine Mother, and Mother Earth herself as well as various angelic beings, including Archangels; Ariel, Gabriel, Michael and other Guides such as WuLan, a Tibetan Master teacher. Divine Mother is especially focused on the reality of living on the Earth in the groups I offer and in this book. She shares how we need to treat her differently with more respect. She also shares the fact that we don't treat her as women are sometimes badly treated in a human relationships.

This book shares how any of us can communicate with Divine Mother by relating to her in nature. It is a collection of true stories and channeled events about how Divine Mother, Star Woman, and Mother Earth herself, communicate with me and through me when I channel. This book also tells the story of how she has guided me as a channel for Divine Spirits to be shared with a larger public.

My wish is to help others learn to listen to her, and relate to her in harmony and love for our future survival and blessings. The following story is one of the many ways she has spoken to me.

CHAPTER ONE

Divine Mother, How to Listen and Speak to Her for Our Future Sustainability and Peace

One day in 2020, during the pandemic, I got a ‘nudge’ to get in my car and drive, then walk to the ocean on the west side of Santa Cruz, CA. I have lived in Santa Cruz County for over twenty-five years. Divine Mother guided me to the cliff's edge on the Pacific Ocean to a shaded public gazebo, where I had a 180 degree view of the Pacific Ocean in front of me, with the coastal land behind me. Her hand was at my back as I walked along the Pacific Ocean on a road that lead to the gazebo.

Below me beyond the cliff's edge were dozens of tidal pools being explored by a few curious families and stragglers alike. I watched as one man got too close to the edge and got soaked by a sneaker wave. At least he did not get sucked into the ocean!

To my left was a beach full of tourists, enjoying their Sunday afternoon under colorful umbrellas and chasing waves at Natural Bridges State Beach. The groups were ten feet apart as we were all still affected by the pandemic. Pelicans flew in ribbons, and sea gulls in pairs. White caps were further out to sea.

Divine Mother had brought me here to speak to her, and mostly to listen to what she wants to say to all of us. The message came through like a bolt of lightning. I could barely write fast enough as it was so clearly directed by her will.

Divine Mother: “My voice is in the waves crashing on the rocks, the sound of the waters’ surge, in the silence between your breaths. Humans are but one species, and this Earth can no longer tolerate its degradation by this single species. No other species degrades the Earth, taking no responsibility for their actions.

“We, the various beings and aspects of my body, oceans, rocks, rivers, forests can be made whole again if humans listen to me, to us, to this body collective–the Earth.

“Show us you can work cooperatively to save the Earth and it’s diversity.

These whales, dolphins, fish, sea otters, are not just here for your exploitation—and harm—they are here because the Creator deemed it so—killing things randomly is not your work here as humans!

Your work is to work cooperatively with ALL beings including plants and animals and all creatures. Yes, some fish are food, but you must see them regenerating themselves environmentally too!

“Stop your poisons on the land—you can farm without them. Your bodies will be healthier without them, fewer cancers, and diseases.

“This is a stern warning.

“It is wonderful to see so many people enjoying the beach sailing and frolicking in the surf. This is good—And where is the gratitude? Some are truly grateful—others look with an eye to exploit. Do no harm and harm will not be done to you. Exploit this Earth, damage her, and you are deciding how the Earth will continue for generations to come. Do you want your grandchildren's children to live in turbulent weather and life threatening danger every season?

"The time has come to decide—Do you love the very Mother you are sustained by? Or do you continue to harm her by your life styles and disregard?

"This Earth is Divine Mother's body. Show some gratitude—some humility—some respect—and you will have the paradise you were promised. No one has expelled you from any garden. You live in it! This is the very garden you were promised. Like disrespectful children some of you have degraded this sacred place.

"I have asked this woman who has demonstrated her love of the Mother to write this book to you, for you—all of you humans—to understand what is at stake. The time is now.

"Love your Mother in all her forms—the oceans, rivers, caves, mountains, valleys desserts fields, and all will be well. Listen to what needs to happen. Listen, then act unto the seventh generation."

Your Divine Mother-All-That-Is.

This message was given to me, November 01, 2020.

It was as though she had given us this message, which is a continuation of a book I had started eight years before. At that time, I had gotten a divorce, and moved to Alamo, CA to eventually attend Mills College for an M.F.A. in a writing/poetry program, and to finish my doctorate in Energy Medicine in another school.

I moved into the pool house of a friend's property for a few months, then onto the back part of the property of the same friend who owned a cabin. The cabin was surrounded by redwood trees and had a stable with two horses of hers who also lived in the back part of the property. I loved relating to the horses and taking time to be close to nature. The first year, I had a lot of time to tune in to the environment.

The following several chapters came from that time when I started this book on Divine Mother and how we can relate to Mother Earth. It offers several experiences with the spirits of nature and Mother Earth herself during my time living there. I quote Yogananda often, because I am a devotee of his and all the teachers/guru's that were his predecessors (Jesus Christ, Babaji Krishna, Laheri Moheshi, Swami Sri Yukteshawar, and Divine Mother). I hope you enjoy it and learn from her what is needed now to live in harmony with Mother Gaia.

"Listen"

"Slow Down"

"Start a relationship with what Lives all around you"

"Recognize life force is in everything"

CHAPTER TWO

Her Helpers and The Sacred Mountain

"The ordinary astral universe-not the subtler astral heaven of Hiranyaloka (Illumined Astral Planet)- is peopled with millions of astral beings who have come, more or less recently, from the earth, and also with myriads of fairies, mermaids, fishes, animals, goblins, gnomes, demigods and spirits, all residing on different astral planets in accordance with karmic qualifications. Various spheric mansions or vibratory regions are provided for good and evil spirits. Good ones can travel freely, but the evil spirits are confined to limited zones. In the same way that human beings live on the surface of earth, worms inside soil, fish in water, and birds in air, so astral beings of different grades are assigned to suitable vibratory quarters." [3]

Under a great mountain outside of a town called Alamo, California, lay a tiny cabin. The cabin is part of a larger property with a big house, a swimming pool, and a pool house. In the winter this mountain turns green when it rains and golden brown in the summer heat. It is wild and full of coyotes and mountain lions, quail and wild turkeys. The mountain, named today, Mt. Diablo, has a spirit that is strong and huge! Anyone can feel this presence of the mountain when hiking or visiting on the mountain. I lived in

3 From of the Autobiography of a Yogi, by Paramhansa Yogananda, as taught to him by his teacher, Sri Yuketeshwar, page 402 in the original edition.

the cabin for three and a half years on my friend Dana and Rajn's property.

No one is allowed to build on this sacred mountain because it is too wild. So it is pretty much the way it is and had been for centuries. The First People knew it as, Tuyshtak (pronounced: Two-sh-tak) or 'dawn of time."

Under the presence of this beautiful slope, when the sun sets in the West, the sun shines on Tukshtak as you face it in the East. It makes the mountain look golden and on fire as the Sun reflects its heat on it's slopes. Perhaps that is where the name "dawn of time" came from.

The Native Americans actually gathered on Tuyshtak every summer. There were over twenty-five different tribes that came together to trade animals, and food and handicrafts. The mountain was a peaceful place where Alone, Chumash, and other tribes gathered to trade their baskets, beads, horses, dogs and jewelry, as well as their gatherings to make ceremonies honoring the Earth. Some called the mountain Dog Mountain because of the trade of their animals.

It was a creation mountain for them, that is, they saw the mountain as a place of the birth of creation and the people. This may be because there are two peaks, one that sets beside the other, one peak for the mother of the mountain, and the other for the father mountain. Some of the people's stories go back to the beginning of time. The people lived in harmony with the mountain and the Earth. They did not take more than they needed and they didn't harm the mountain in anyway. The First People also celebrated on the mountain, and gave thanks to it by offering it some of their harvest with small plates of food.

Moving To Mount Tuyshtak

As I settle into my tiny cabin, I noticed all beings live here together in peace even to this day. There are coyotes, mountain lions, and wild turkeys, birds of all kinds including turkey vultures, red tail hawks, and quail, and also mice, raccoons, tree and ground squirrels. Oh, and rattlesnakes!

I have been offering food to the land, to Mother Earth, to the spirit of the forest for some time. I set out small dishes of food from every meal, called 'spirit plates' by some Native American friends who taught me how to do these offerings every day.

Now I have been intending for the food to go to the animals that lived in the woods nearby. But as I realized just the week before, I had not really been connecting with the spirit of the Earth. That is very different I discovered. So instead, I decided to leave the food offering, just a wee bit of everything I ate, to the spirits of the Earth in thanks. It helped me feel more grateful.

So as I gave some food to the mountain and the animals and intended to connect with the spirits of the Earth too, I noticed a deeper feeling of love for my new home.

Just one week after setting my intention to connect, that is when my little friend began to visit me. While I was eating my breakfast one day in my little cabin on the farm where I lived, I suddenly became aware of a presence sitting across from me, his nose just poking over the table.

There in the bench seat was a little man. He was an Elf or Gnome, or a Nisse, as they say in Norway, a spirit of the Earth, or forest. I was surprised and delighted to have him join me.

He wore a little red cap and sported a beard, white of course, and he had a little red suit that he wore with a shirt or blouse underneath with sleeves showing and a collar with a bit of a ruffle around the edge.

He wore boots that curled up on the toes and he had a black belt, pattern leather with a broad buckle. Yes, he looked like a miniature Santa Claus! I remembered that Santa Claus had come from someone's contact with a Gnome in Northern Europe, especially Norway.

Once I got over my surprise with his presence, he said, "Hello!"

I said, "Hello!"

There he was talking to me like anyone else would.

I asked him if he would like some of my breakfast. He said, "Yes, that would be lovely."

So after offering him some food after a long pause, I asked him "What can I do for you?"

He said between bites, "Write our meeting and our friendship as a story so others will know."

"Oh" I said. "Hmm. I'll have to think about that."

"Yes, please do!" he replied. "You have free will, just know that I am here and would love to connect with you and have you write about it."

It didn't take me long to realize what he was asking.

Suddenly, I saw a book in the offing. This book. It came to my mind as a picture book. This picture book!

"I see," I said to him. "You want me to write a book about my relationship to the spirits of the land, including the Mountains and the elementals, yes?"

"Precisely." he said.

"Give me some time." I asked.

"Of course." he said. "I have been waiting 800 years or so, another few weeks won't matter."

A few days later he came by again and after greeting each other, and sharing some food with him. I said, "Yes, okay, I will."

He was very pleased and then he added, "…and paint us too."

"Paint?" I said.

"Yes, you know, paint my picture."

Then he turned in his seat and struck a pose for me in profile and smiled with a very wide grin, I began to laugh. "Okay, I said, it would be my pleasure."

We launched into this project together, me and my new friend the Gnome.

The next night the Spirit of Mount Tuyshtak came to visit. He was huge and could not fit inside my little house. He was so big and came in to say hello though he couldn't really stay long. Then he spoke to me in a very low deep voice.

"Because you are at the foot of the Mountain and because it is winter, and everything sleeps, I can come visit you."

"I love you great mountain." I said, for I did. "Thank you for your presence in my life."

He said, "I feel your love and, you know, I love you too." He rested his huge hand against the door frame of my house and I touched his finger and he replied in a low vibrant, "Thank you."

The Spirit of Mount Tuyshtak left, and let me know he was there for me.

"And please visit soon." He said.

The next night, the little man sat across from me as he did the morning before.

"We want to keep talking to you." He said.

"Yes!" I said, with enthusiasm. "And I am happy to talk with you too!"

So that is how this book began. All of this book contains true stories. Nothing is made up, it is just recorded for your understanding of the spirits of nature.

The little man and I watched a movie together that night. We saw; Wild Nature.

Offering of food to Mother Gaia in Gratitude

CHAPTER THREE

Meeting Mo's Family

Bindy, Mo, Laurisa and Big Mo

The next morning the little man, who called himself a Gnome, came to visit again and we ate breakfast as we had before, offering him a little bit of my food from my plate onto a special plate for him and his family.

No sooner did I have the thought "his family" than he ushered in his wife and two children.

"We want to formerly welcome you to this place." He announced.

Here are my wife and children.

"Thank you!" I said. "How did you come here?"

"We came when they planted these trees." He pointed out the window to the redwoods outside the window. The trees, planted by the previous owner, had been planted about ten years before their giant house was built. The redwoods were above us on a small cliff face about six feet high. The current house was at least ten years old.

The gnome's wife was round and happy little woman. She seemed delighted to be with us. The children giggled and poked each other playfully.

"So you came with the trees?" I inquired.

"Yes." was all he had to say. Then he took a breath. "You see they have a very large house on this property, but the trees bring it more into balance with the land."

"I hope I haven't intruded too much on your place by living here." I said.

"There are more people living on this land than ever before." He said seriously, "But we are happy to share with you."

"Thank you," I said.

"You are a pleasure, because you know we are here, and you love the mountain." He said grinning.

"Yes, I do," I said with a smile and warmth in my heart.

"Soon, more people will know about us. This is good." He said.

"What are you names? I asked. All of them giggled together. Their laughter sounded like gurgling stream.

"This is Bindy, and Mo our children." Bindy was the girl and Mo a boy.

"And your name my friend?"

Up to then, the little man refused to tell me his name. He avoided it at every turn. I seemed to remember something about how a Queen had to guess the name of Rumpelstiltskin to keep her child.

His wife then spoke up, then paused, as if to see if I were trustworthy.

"My name is Laurisssssa." She threw her head back and offered her name with a grin and great pleasure, in profile of course, extending the 's' with a flair.

I said, "Thank you, Laurisa, it's nice to know your name."

"And yours?" I implored her husband. He was getting off the seat and his family followed.

"You can call me Big Mo, Mo for short." His children giggled as they left through the door without opening it. Somehow I knew it was not his real name. But I liked it just the same.

"Big Mo it is!" I called after him.

"Bindy, Mo, Laurisa and Big Mo." I repeated and grabbed my journal to write down their names. "Good bye see you later!"

We were off to a fine start, I thought.

CHAPTER FOUR

Giant Lessons from Big Mo

Mo came in the next morning as I was eating breakfast. I greeted him and then I offered him some toast with jam as usual as an offering, and he accepted it.

Then he said: "I want to bring to you a bigger understanding about what is happening in the Earth. There is a big change occurring right now,

and we want you to know you will help others understand it.

"What we want you to know, even though your life looks very solitary, is that it is not. We are here, and part of why you seem to be alone is to turn towards the spirits of the Earth and Sky to help you grow.

"We love you, and wish you to know we are here to help you write this book. We know you understand too."

"Have there been no other humans who have come to you?" I felt so sad.

"Well, we have many Shaman's and other First People who are closer to the Earth than others. But as far as most people from your culture, no, I am sad to say, very few." Big Mo looked down at his hands, and I felt his saddness too.

"But that is your job! To wake them up!" Mo said and lit the room with his smile.

"Yes, I see that." I said shrinking under the weight of the task.

"Don't worry," he said, "We are here. We will help you."

"So Big Mo, please tell me, what do you want people to know about you and the Earth Spirit World?"

"Well, the most important thing I want to tell everyone is that we can save the planet and people from destruction. Only if human's start cooperatively working with the Earth Mother, and us, she will not have to react to the destructive tendencies of some of your people."

"But Mo, who are you? What kind of spirit are you?" I said with some curiosity.

“Wow, I guess I need to start at the beginning.” Mo said holding his head and walking in circles.

“I am, there really is no ‘I’ here, that is to say, I am not what you think. I am Big Mo, keeper of trees for this region.” He said standing up erect. “You would call me a Gnome, but we are not just little spirits that play in the trees. We work cooperatively with the other beings of the Earth, Gnomes, Trolls, Divas, and Fairies. We are here to keep some things wild and according to the laws of Nature.

“Trolls protect areas of the Earth. Gnomes protect groves of trees and regions where similar vegetation lives, Divas are what you might call Goddesses and protect whole areas of trees like an entire forest or the atmosphere, a storm system, or water shed. Fairies, and Elves protect and help individual plants.

“Mother Nature is a real being of Light. Her service is to help people grow, by giving them a place to live their lives. She is so beautiful and loving. She is also clearly harsh for those not awake to her power.

“All people need to do is be grateful to her, to show some gratitude and love for being provide for so completely. Everything you human's have, comes from the Earth. Is it too much to just offer a thank you?"

I could see that Big Mo was very sad about the lack of gratitude that humans offer the Earth. I felt sad too.

"This practice you do, of offering a bit from the meal, where did you learn this?" Mo inquired.

"It is how we begin each meal, with the teachings of the Native people who I have gone to dances with in South Dakota, Wisconsin, and Washington State. We put food out to offer back to the Earth what we have created from her bounty. What we make, a casserole, pudding, or bread, we offer it back after we have transformed the wheat or berries, or cheese into food we eat."

"Exactly, this is a good practice and the spirits of nature, and Mother Nature herself appreciate it as gratitude. Now you changed a few weeks ago, when you felt the connection you made with the Earth, and moved from your heart with your small offering, isn't that correct?" Mo said.

"Yes." I said sheepishly. " I realized that even I, who knew the practice of offering, had not really been connecting to the Earth from my heart. So I changed my attitude and began to offer it in desire to connect with the spirit of the Mother, and of the Mountain. And here you are. And then the Mountain's spirit came last week too!"

"Exactly, you made a shift, and all the offerings you had made were received differently after that. We heard your heart. The Mother Earth speaks heart language.

"If people sincerely want to help, they can, but their actions must start with speaking from the Heart. The heart connects all things. It connects our love, and fears and heart ache and anger too. Humans have to come to the Mother Earth empty, realizing they don't know as much as they think they know. That is why it becomes important to sincerely ask from the Heart. Love is not only what created this Earth, it is what sustains it."

"Thank you, Mo. I am very touched by what you have shared with me. It helps me so much."

"We want people of the world and especially children to know that this Divine Mother Earth hears their every thought, their every internal question, their every desire and attitude. We know what needs healing, and what doesn't. How do we do this? We are not spying, we are listening to the Earth itself, to their bodies. Their bodies are the Earth itself! So you see there is no escaping the Earth while you are here. When your spirit leaves the Earth, part of you, your body, returns and what is imprinted in your spirit is the record of how you lived your life. Not what was accomplished, as much as how you felt, and lived and were in your actions and attitudes with others—your being. Are you being love or fear, love or anger, love or arrogance, love or harming others with your thoughts or actions?

"I want people to know that the Earth is an Angel come to help. She is a Diva, and she is a Saint, and a Gnome, and a Bear, and a Human, she is all of it. She has agreed to help humanity grow into more of itself. So first she made a shift, now it is human's turn to shift. That is where we are now. The problem is, while some are moving, others are STUCK!"

"Yes, they are. But that is where healing comes in." I smiled.

"Yes, and some people will hold fast to their beliefs so tight, that they will stop their growth. But we want to help people understand that EVERYTHING is connected. Great saints and hardened criminals are all connected. Whether they are connected to you is dependent on your thoughts and your actions. So think good thoughts, and you will be happier. Think about love, and be the love that you are, and you will be happier. Connect with the spirits of Nature and we can help you feel loved, because you are. You are never alone."

"Thank you Mo. Yes, I feel that, even when I am alone with no other humans, I hear and feel and see you. It helps me feel less separate."

"That is the very point I am trying to make. You are NOT separate. But sometimes people feel separate. That is what needs healing, the feeling of separation."

"Yes, I could not agree more." I said.

"You see we are all here for the same reason: To LOVE everything, AND to recognize that love is you too. Life current is a loving current. It comes from Nature all around you. It comes from great beings, and everything here is love. It comes from other humans and animals too. The love I am talking about is like a unconditional love-filled, great river.

"People get off track. That is what has happened to humanity at this time and I hope I help you get on track. The track of healing separation, to being in Love is the right track for everyone. Loving your being, loving the Earth, seeing that the Earth is precious, this is the change that is needed to save humanity and the Earth."

"Mother Earth, Gaia, she is precious because she loves you. She loves all beings. She is love, loving through you. Mother Earth's body is your body. And all that is required is for people to recognize that they are in a field of love and attune to that. It is really simple. But to do that, they need these important keys:

1) slow down
2) listen
3) recognize other's life force in plants, trees, animals. Life force is in everything
4) Start a relationship with what lives around you
5) Ask Mother Earth for help
6) Be willing to receive it
7) Ask her what she needs from you, right where you are
8) Exchange help and see that you can effect change right in your own home
9) Be grateful, and offer gratitude through everything you eat
10) Love her and love yourself as a being of love
11)

"Wow Mo, that is great! Thank you. I can feel how different that is from rushing around, and what is needed to help us right wherever we are."

"Yes, well there is more." He said.

Then he scooted off the bench seat and walked out of my cabin.

"We will talk more tomorrow." He said.

Spirit of the Forest

Rainbow Woman

CHAPTER FIVE

Meeting Mother Gaia

When Mo returned the next day, he was a bit grumpy.

"What's going on Mo?" I asked as I shared a piece of toast with him.

"Thank you, the toast tastes delicious, is there any jam?" Mo asked.

I brought out the raspberry jam and sat across from him at the table with my breakfast, spreading some jam on his toast.

Mo was quiet as he ate his toast and jam.

"I have been thinking of what you said yesterday, Mo, about how to connect with our life force with the Earth. How the Mother Earth is our body! Our spirits are Love. That is quite an amazing thought. Then I started thinking about how far we are from that."

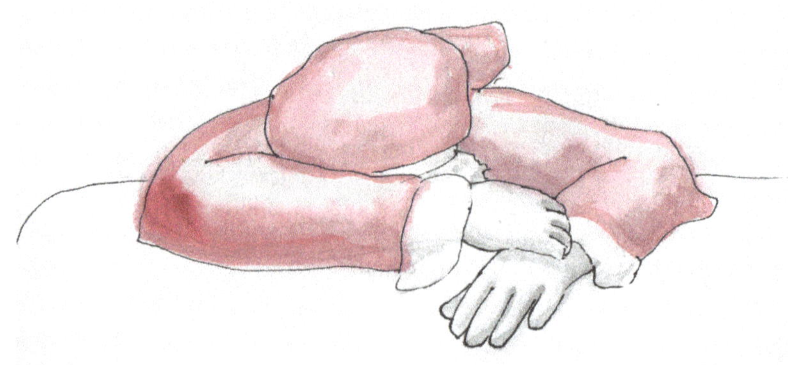

"Exactly. You humans haven't gotten it yet! I am rather sad today about it."

Mo placed his head on the table nestled in one arm.

"Oh Mo, don't worry. The Mother Earth will take care of herself. And I believe people are beginning to wake up."

"It would help if people relied on their heart experiences rather than their rational brains." Mo said. "You see, all of nature works together for the good of all beings on the Earth, human and otherwise. But some humans see themselves as separate and superior and do not see that their thoughts and emotions affect the weather and harm the Earth.

"You have been seeing our communities of little beings, Elves, Fairies, Gnomes, and Divas, since you were a baby. But most people block it out or become afraid. That is so sad. Usually their parents get afraid, and transfer it to the kids. But there is nothing to be afraid of. We are here to help people live a more connected life, a better life. We are here to help the vegetables and flowers grow more abundantly!"

"What do you, or Mother Earth, want in return, Mo?"

"We only want you humans to recognize our existence—that we are real." Mo replied.

"People get so busy in their minds, and think they have to do, do, do all the time. What I am suggesting is that they stop and smell the jasmine flowers. Then stop and feel into the reality of us there, helping the plants and animals. We are here to serve and learn from human beings."

"It seems humans need to learn from you first!" I said quietly.

"Well, perhaps." Mo said. "I want to have you meet… to show you … something, someone... Are you willing?"

"Yes," I said. "What is it you want me to see?"

At that, Mo's mood changed into a bright sunny Mo that I had known when he first arrived. He jumped off the seat and landed on the floor, and went quickly out the door.

"Follow me!" He said.

I went outside, and he asked me to lay in my hammock so my body could relax, while he guided my spirit into the Earth.

"Right this way," he said to my spirit.

I could feel my spirit rise and follow him. Mo raised his hand and made a circle in the air. Suddenly a round door appeared. We traveled through the round doorway as it opened into the Earth, and inside was a trail that moved past his underground home. I waved at his family standing outside, as we passed his house door. We stayed on the main trail inside the Earth. But we did not have to walk, we floated and flew down and in, into the center of the Earth!

Soon we came to another doorway, and inside that door, was a cave like room. In the center of the room was a fireplace. From behind the fire came a beautiful woman. She was glowing, a vibrant spirit, dressed in a robe of many colors swirling and coursing through her gown. The robe was trimmed in gold. She had a sweet disposition, a very gentle spirit. Yet I could tell she was no one to lie to, nor to try and fool. I felt her gaze go right through me. Her skin was blue.

Mo removed his hat, showing his nearly baldhead and bowed a low bow.

I knelt before her, out of respect, for I knew it was the Spirit of the

Mother Earth herself.

“Good day, Robin White Turtle Woman. I have asked Mo to bring you to my chamber, so that you can see that I am real.”

“This is a rare audience, I wish you to know this, but since you have maintained your innocence, even through the difficulties you have had in your life, and you are of the Turtle Clan, those who can travel from one world to another, from water and air, and inside the Earth, I wish for you to take my message to the people of Earth.”

Yes, Dear Mother Gaia. Anyway I can be of service. I am here to help.” I said to the spirit of the Earth as I rose and bowed my head to her.

As I watched her, and dared look at her, she changed her form from young beauty to an old woman, and back again. Her robes went from white, with gold trim, to multicolored, to dark when she started sharing the sadness she had."

"My flowers and trees and animals are so beautiful. How they interweave their life force, as I share the bounty of my realm with all. Amazing how creatures adjust to climate depending on the location of the surface. This is because of my many beings working to support life. Fairies help flowers and plants, Elves help the trees and flowerless plants, Gnomes protect large areas of land, and spirits of all kinds work with me cooperatively to support and sustain life on my bodily surface. Trolls protect groves of trees and rivers. Mo is a Gnome that protects the grove of trees that were planted and he maintains the forest in the area where you live.

"But my beings, and humans too, are suffering from the disrespect humans are showing to surface of my body. The Earth is a gift, but not a gift to take for granted. We of the Earth realms know that the time has come to cleanse and renew. We are preparing. We must if we are to have future life on my sacred body. All Mothers, any mother, simply needs respect, love and consideration. Greed cannot be the motivation to take from me. Gratitude is the way."

There was a long silence. Then she said quietly, "Please take this to the surface and share my message."

"But Mother, isn't there more required from humanity? Just respect, love and gratitude?" I said in protest. What of restoration, what of honoring life, what about strip mining, what of plastics in the ocean, what of the pollution, deforestation…"

Mother Earth raised her hand to silence me.

"Dear one, we see your passion to help restore the body of my realm. But we want you to see that if humans have respect, love and gratitude, and consider what they use every day, they will be less likely to harm me or my creatures. They may even see me as sacred, as precious to them. They will receive rather than take, out of their entitled attitude, as if it was theirs to grab. Everything is a gift!" She said slowly.

She paused and came towards me from the fireplace and took my hand. I felt a current of energy filling me from her touch. It was a sweet loving current that filled me with life force energy. I felt old, stuck, locked up energy fly away! What remained was my spirit full of vibrancy and love.

"Dear one, you see that my Earth body is fully capable of healing itself,

as I have just healed you. Yet, if a miner or a tree cutter, or a man who works on oil drilling platforms, thanks the very soil, oil, minerals and plants that bring them sustenance and puts food on their tables, if fishermen and women thank the fish, the waters, and all life, sincerely from their hearts, this would turn around the desperate situation human's find themselves in currently, where they have disregarded the Mother, their Mother and taken without giving something in return. Life itself is thrown out of balance. Taking without permission goes against the laws of free will and disrespects the very Mother you have all come from.

"This is all I ask in return: love, respect and gratitude, and deep regard for what you use. Ask without taking, love from the heart, and say thank you. Small children learn this in kindergarten, do they not?"

"Yes, Mother, they do. I thank you for this message, and I promise I will deliver it to whomever I can." I said.

"One more thing, dear one. If they work with the spirits of nature, like they have in many large gardens, like Findhorn and other communities, as many gardeners do, love of the Earth will be easier to sustain human life."

"Yes, Mother. I will tell them." I said.

"This is shared out of love, not that I have to, or that I really desire to save the human race. Some of the humans who care about water, or air or earth will survive. I share this because I want to give humans one more chance to see their destructive ways and make this apparent small change.

Be grateful, recognize the spirits of the land and work cooperatively with them. You may not see them, but feel them. They are there; in the rivers, in the ocean, in the forest, in the grasses, in the soil. Everywhere.

"I wish you to visit my friend in the Mountain. He has much to teach you. Then you will be ready." She said as she turned back to the fire. "I do not want to have to cleanse the surface of the human race entirely. It has never been part of MY plan. But humanity leaves me no choice." At that she turned dark with sadness and anger.

"But you my dear, and others like you, can bring my message to them. She then grew into her radiant self and swirled into a column of light and disappeared. The fire grew bright then went back to a steady low flame.

I stood with Mo, and he with me, and I melted into a heap on the floor. My hands over my face, I began to weep.

"Oh Mo, what if they don't wake up. What shall I do?" I cried.

"Do not worry. It is not all on you. There are many of us working to change." Mo said. As he said that, I could see before me many light-filled people who loved the Earth sprinkled everywhere around me. They were like a sea of love all around the Earth.

"Come now, it is time to return." Mo said.

As soon as he said it, we rose and were lifted through the same door. Then we floated through the tunnel we moved through before and popped out on the surface. My spirit went back into my body, and as if I awoke from a dream, I sat up in my hammock.

Mo was gone, but the memory of the Mother stayed with me, as well as her request. "Tell them: Be grateful, recognize the spirits of the land and work cooperatively with them."

CHAPTER SIX

Meeting the Spirit of Mt. Tuyshtak Again

A few days later, as I was writing down my talk with her and grappling with her messages that I was to deliver to everyone else, I drove to visit the mountain. I decided to spend the weekend camping there and set up my camp over looking the valley.

After I got set up, I sat on the edge of a cliff, and began to go inside my heart. In one meditation, I felt the spirit of the Mountain alive and standing before me. He took my spirit's hand and brought me to a doorway that appeared suddenly. He showed me the place where he lives and brought me deep, deep, deep into the mountain depth. We came to a chamber, where a golden thrown stood and glowed. He took his seat at the thrown and then he said to me:

"This is who you are." He pointed to himself then the golden thrown where he sat, and asked me to sit there. Then he said:

"Be the Mountain that you are. Be clear and strong, and know you are Love itself."

As I sat on his thrown, I felt a kind of power that I had never felt before,

What is a mountain? A large place on the Earth that shelters many, and

helps people be all they can be. At least that seemed to be what I was here to do. Help others heal their lives, to stand in their power so they can be their best selves.

"Everyone has an affinity with an element, earth, air, water or fire in their heart center. Some burn with light, others are solid and secure as the Earth, still others are water or air. Each brings something vital to all others and feeds others. Each needs the other." The Spirit of Mountain Tuyshkak said.

Over the next few days camping, I enjoyed the Fairies, Elves on the Mountain face, and shooed the raccoons away from my picnic table.

Racoons and Fairy
with Gnome

Yellow Fairy

Purple Fairy

Jack the Gnome

Divine Mother Image

CHAPTER SEVEN

Mo Speaks to Me

Over the next two years, I made regular visits to the Mountain alone and with friends. Then came a time to leave my little cabin, and move back to where I had lived before in Santa Cruz, CA.

I told Mo what I was doing, and to my surprise he already knew.

"Yes, you are being guided. It is time for you to find your place away from here." Mo said. "Go and don't forget your promise!"

It seemed as though my life turned over and over after that. My search for my place in the world took me back to a land I had lived in before, in the mountains then along the coast, and I was happy to return to my coastal home of Santa Cruz County. I missed Mo, but he told me after we visited the Mother Earth's chamber, that he would always be near, just by thinking of him and he would come to me on the "Inner Earth Express."

Several years past, I could smell the salt air, and hear people walking, and enjoying life in a park nearby in Santa Cruz. Soon, I was busy with my counseling business, and forgot about my promise, until one day, I was settling into my 3rd new home, which I felt I would be in more than a year or two, and I opened a file that contained the pictures of Mo and his family, which he had asked me to paint of them. Mo seemed to speak to me through the picture.

"Remember your promise."

I did remember, and found this story to share with you. So that is why I am writing this book for you, readers, so you can go outside and listen to the Earth Mother through the trees and flowers, through her workers, Fairies, Elves, Trolls and Gnomes, keepers of areas of Earth, and the Mother Ocean, Mother River, talk to them, offer them love, gratitude, and respect. Give a rose, or few strands of your hair, some corn meal, a small amount from your plate, or just your love, and see how you might open a conversation that they have been waiting to have with you for centuries.

It maybe the beginning of a new / ancient way of living and affirming life itself!

Portal
Acrylic on canvas

CHAPTER EIGHT

Reconnecting to Mother Earth

After my meeting with Mother Earth by the ocean on the west side of Santa Cruz, I felt the pressure from her wanting me to write this down. I released my forgetfulness and I began to write some thoughts about what she had said to me.

I was feeling overwhelmed by finding ways to present this information. I realized through my love of Mother Earth, that we cannot live here without the Earth. Period. Our bodies are the Earth. Being here is an opportunity to find a way to live in harmony between our spirits and our physical form and with each other in peace. We are here also for our spiritual growth to become one with All-That-Is. We need to learn what we must in a body in Schoolhouse Earth. Then our souls will live on after death after we leave our bodies.

Another message I received a few weeks after this conversation with Mother Gaia, came from Divine Mother, the over arching spirit of Creation:

Divine Mother: "Covid-19 and its variants are here because in many parts of the world, humans have not really turned inwards to discover an inner life, and through inward inquiry and exploration we discover that humans are one with all life."

Everyone has and can have a connection with Divine Mother. I am not at all exceptional in that regard. The book also gives ways to connect and listen to her in nature every day through true stories I have to share. When I get these instructions, I listen, because I have learned that the world needs what she is offering us through her grace.

I hope this book finds its way into as many people's hands and hearts as possible so they can hear what she has been saying, for sometime, to

Golden Portal - Acrylic on canvas

many of us who love Divine Mother. For those who listen, I am grateful, because together we must change as a species to love the Mother Earth and work with her, not against her. We can have a personal relationship with her, and we must develop one with her, or we will not survive the coming global-wide changes without it.

Divine Mother lives everywhere, in the flower, in the face of a child or any loved one, in every person, in every animal, plant and in the stars and galaxies. This is the essence of every spiritual teaching on the planet. How do we realize that we are a wonderful part of creation itself?

Teachings from all over the world point to our inward relationship and how this idea is a reality when we focus. From Indigenous teachings to Hindu, Buddhist, and Islamic teachings, from various African tribal teachings to that of the wisdom of any Earth-based philosophy all speak of what the Creator has given us and how to live in gratitude with the Mystery.

This book is a book for emerging the new age, as we are living In it now. It is a road map for moving from self-destructive actions against the Earth and all species, towards bringing what we already know from various traditions into practice, to help the Earth and all the creatures living on it.

It will hopefully redefine our priorities to help us all live on Mother Earth in a sustainable, reverent and creative way. I offer it as a way forward and hope for the future unto the seventh generation.

CHAPTER NINE

Many ways that Divine Mother Speaks through Her Guidance for Us and through Gaia

"If we approach nature with love, it will serve us as our best friend, a friend that won't let us down."
"Love is our true Nature."
Amma

Mother Earth Speaks to Us

Listening to Divine Mother, no matter how she manifests, whether as Amma, or Pele, or as a Mother Tree, Star Woman, Mother Mary, or Divine Mother who speaks through our hearts, she gives us new perspective that comes through to help us.

When Mother Earth speaks to those who listen, she often has poignant things to say that brings us into a greater understanding of our own existence. Often her loving way of being is felt with her dialog.

The Mother Earth is a Living Being

Since I was a small child, I have been talking to the Mother Earth. Sometimes it was through pets or animals that lived around me. Many people talk with their pets.

When I was very small, my older sisters made doors where the fairies lived at the base of the trees in front of our grandmother's house in Evanston, Illinois. My sisters and I connected with the tree's spirit, and I saw the actual fairies.

Growing up in the Lutheran church, I remember seeing; Father, Son and Holy Ghost on the front of the lectern. I was upset that they discounted Divine Mother. "Where is the woman's place in the sacred triangle?" I remember saying to myself at age 15. I was appalled at it. Later I remember learning that the triangle was symbolic of the feminine, and that the Holy Ghost was the feminine Divine Mother, it was reinterpreted by the patriarchy as all male aspects of the Divine.

As I got older, into my late 20's, I lived in Michigan with my first husband in an old Grist Mill that we bought from his brother. I loved the place, and it had a pond and a creek beside it. Once, when I was on a small bridge that crossed the creek to an old storage shed, I felt the creek speak to me in a loving and harmonious way. I felt myself flooded with light. I remember feeling the love of Nature flow through me. I sat down on the bridge, and felt the light pouring through me like a waterfall.

Many times throughout my lifetime, talking to trees was natural. I would lean up against them, and they would greet me. Rocks too. The first time I leaned on a boulder in Yosemite National Park, the Rock said, "Hellooo dearrrr one." The voice was male, and very deep and slow. I was shocked, but then I rested on it and said, "Hello dear Rock." I could feel its love and warmth. I was delighted. Then I laid my hands and my cheek on it. I could feel the embrace of nature. I continued down the trail and saw a brown bear crossing the trail to enjoy a bunch of apple trees full of fruit. I stopped on the trail, watching the bear one-hundred feet or more away, and felt it was an affirmation of my connection with Mother Earth.

When I started in my twenties and thirties to attend Native American sacred sweat lodges, I felt the connection even more deeply. As I started offering sweat lodge ceremonies in my forties after being a Sun Dancer in my late thirties and forties, A Mother Tree near my lodge became part of my life. Every time I would get ready for the lodge, I would touch the Mother Tree that was standing over our lodge, and felt her love, affirmation and blessings. I offered her some tobacco and gratitude watching over us, and she would hear the prayers and I felt her love over us.

My 2nd husband and I often went to the ocean to receive clearing, rest, and regeneration. We were happy to receive the healing from the Mother Ocean. He and I attended Earth-based Annishnabe ceremonies in Wisconsin, Brazilian Umbanda ceremonies in Santa Cruz, CA, and also visited the Umbanda Center in Sao Paulo, Brazil with Pai Carlos Buby, the Babalorixá, or the main Priest of this sect.

The ocean is known in Umbanda as 'the great cemetery,' because when someone is lost at sea, they are rarely recovered. This also is true for emotions we want to release, and parts of our past.

At the end of our relationship, when he decided to move back to Puerto Rico after his retirement (we were 14 years apart and I had just gotten my private practice going after ten years of effort), we went to the ocean at Seabright Beach where we often went, and I gave our relationship to the Mother Ocean. I felt he was doing the same thing, even though we did not talk about what we were communicating individually with her. It felt right and important, because our karma was ending.

Today, many years later as an intuitive/medium, I do many things for people, and one of them is clearing houses. When I do house clearings of negative spirits and entities, I look for a tree on the property, and ask the tree, after offering tobacco, to let me know about the history of the property and the house. It always lets me know, as trees are witnesses to history of a particular location. They know and tell me what the Native Americans used the land for, whether it was pass through area, ceremonial area, or villages, before any western or Mexican settlers came to the land. If someone died, there are spirits guarding the burial ground. The trees tell me about the land and aspects of the Native people who lived here for centuries. Confirmation of what they tell me comes through my intuition, and I understand what is needed to clear or negotiate with the entities that live on the property.

The Mother Earth gives us everything we need to live. Living food, clothing, shelter, cars, trucks and anything you want to create. She is a living presence, and very advanced and compassionate being. How do we know this? It is so obvious that life and love cannot spring from what we might consider emptiness!

She gives all of us, no matter who we are, no matter our social or material status, room to grow through life lessons by the choices we make every day. She gives us room to make mistakes, and correct them, she gives us a place to learn, the same as any benevolent, compassionate mother would. Our spirits have a home in our temple bodies, and for that we can be very grateful.

Our bodies are the Earth, as Mo stated and Mother Earth told us, as they are made of Earth's elements, and need the elements to survive and thrive. We eat foods that contain minerals for our bones and muscles, the air we must breathe, water we must drink daily, and the fire of our digestion. We consume planets and animals, or food that we use to help ourselves live

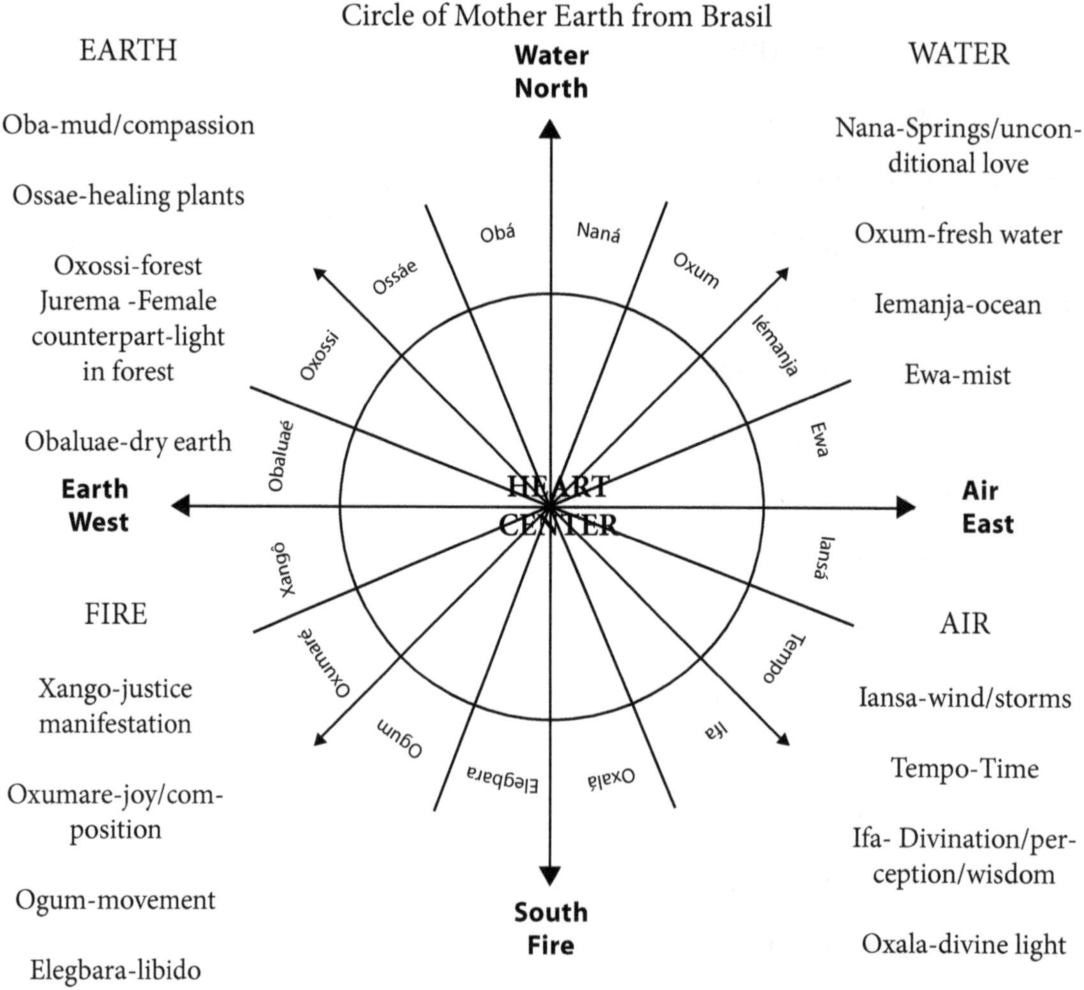

and thrive. We cannot live without the Mother Earth providing all of this for us. *What we do to the Earth, we do to ourselves.*

Beyond the physical reality of food and water to survive, each person has a dominant element that they express as part of their fundamental essence. These essential elements are called Orixás. These elements are Earth, Air, Fire, and Water and combinations of the elements. Think about people that you could name who are fiery, or who are earthy, or very grounded, and others who have an affinity towards water, or air as their primary element. Being with these elements as us, is not something that most westerners are familiar with, but it is something to consider. The Spirit of each element is our essences and reflects our souls.

Other cultures know this very well, from Indigenous people from all around the world, to African-based Condomblé, and Umbanda, spiritual traditions in Brazil, and all over the Caribbean (Santeria, and other traditions based on Yoruba traditions), as well as in Africa in many parts of the Eastern African continent. Different areas have the directions and elements in different locations depending on where they live on the planet.

Also Mother Nature is infused in Eastern traditions, such as in Japan through the Shinto tradition, and other Eastern indigenous traditions focus on nature as a spirit and an element of love. East Indian elements are expressed in Kali, and other Divine Mother images, as well as the sacred rivers. Ancient Nordic Gods are also based on natural elements, as were the Greek Gods and Goddesses. Even in the Buddhist tradition, they have the same eight teachings that are symbolized by a medicine wheel with the four directions (east, south, west and north) and quarter directions (northeast, southeast, southwest, and northwest) as well as the center (heart) and the circle, which is All-That-Is. We simply cannot divorce ourselves from the Earth no matter where we are from around the world. Enlightened beings know this and see the Earth as sacred Divine Mother.

We can evolve out of the Earth when we become enlightend. That is another service the Earth does for us as Schoolhouse Earth.

Pele, Mother Volcano

On a recent trip to Hawaii, I visited the Kilauea volcano, and walking near her caldera, a sign said, "Be aware that Pele, the spirit of volcanoes in Hawaii, might speak to you." I was delighted that a National Park informs people of the Native Hawaiian people's understanding and that they still practice their traditions, and their understanding of nature. It was letting people know they also might experience her.

I walked out to a ledge that looked over her caldera, and offered a few strands of my hair to speak to her. The wind picked up the hair and blew my offering down into the smoky bubbling area at her core. I felt her come to me, as though she was active and preparing for more activity. Pele and I connected because she is my Orixá, or the essence of my internal energy. This is what she said to me:

Pele: "What people don't know is that volcanic movement happens everywhere, and there could easily be eruptions anywhere. Just so you know! Those eruptions are not to harm but to create! They are focused on making more Earth that could be lived on eventually, as well as extending the land.

"People are focused on their present lives, but existence is much bigger than that. Everyone has many lives and many more reformations. Fire is not anger; fire is regeneration! It ends and begins things. The functional foundation of the Earth is created by this expansion. Let it move and let you move forward with it."[4]

After I left the caldera, she erupted. When I made it back to my hotel, I felt Mother Pele's fiery energy moving through me burning up whatever I did not need any longer. Her love and clarity renewed my inner self.

My Lakota Story

Many years ago, my experiences with Native traditions started when I was in college my sophomore year. I was invited by a dear friend, Mary Ann Godfrey, to visit her in South Dakota. She happened to be a Native American Lakota woman who I graduated with from Kemper Hall, in Kenosha, WI.

When I visited her two years after we graduated, she surprised me with a sacred sweat lodge to honor our friendship. I was so grateful.

Twelve years after undergraduate school I went to graduate school. I met Buck Ghosthorse who taught at The Institute of Culture and Creation Spirituality where I was attending Mathew Fox's Graduate program on cultural change. I was also meditating, learning from Da Free John, and practicing my Christian values of love, peace and harmony.

---

4 Pele is the spirit of volcanic eruption in the Kilauea volcano on the Big Island. When I was there on vacation recently, I spoke to her spirit, and this was what she said to me.

A few years later, I was invited to a Sundance on the Rosebud Lakota Sioux Indian reservation. After school, I moved to Marin County north of San Francisco. I started attending sweat lodges with a Native American women who ran a lodge up near Sebastapol, and I was praying and singing the songs with Buck in California and Washington State in various ceremonies in the Lakota tradition. But I had never been to such a dance on the reservation.

When I arrived on the reservation in South Dakota, several years after moving to California, I was shocked to see at least five-hundred people gathered from all over the country, some even from Europe and Mexico. Many Lakota people were coming home to their home base to take part in this renewal ceremony. Others were supporters helping out. I was with my own "tribe" of friends from graduate school. We had bonded as a family, and were part of each other's extended family. Many people from my hometown of Rockford, Illinois were also there. They were friends of my extended family from graduate school and my childhood church.

That ceremony changed my life. So many pieces that did not make sense in the Lutheran church I had grown up in, were clearer to me and acknowledged as sacred in this ceremony. This included honoring the Mother Earth.

The first thing that excited me was that it was held outside in a large tree arbor instead of an enclosed stone church. The earth, sky and center of the medicine wheel or the wheel of life, were the configuration of the dance grounds, a circle with an equidistant cross, designating the four directions, the four races of all people, the four seasons, and the four elements.

Everything that was part of the ceremony, from sage that was burned to clear the air and bring in positive energy, to the tree of life that was danced around, brought together heaven and earth and the heart. The people had built it, and the people were embodying prayer by physical sacrifice. The dancers fasted and ate or drank nothing for four days. Their faith sustained them and the prayers of supporters kept them going.

At that dance I discovered aspects of creation that are clearly presented in these ways through various dancers. Some dancers embodied change as a part of the world as they brought in joy and the reality of death. They were called Hayokas, and have other names in other traditions. (Windigo in Annishabe or Ojibway traditions, the court jester in traditional monarchies of Europe.)

I saw a dance that was sacred as our own lives are sacred. This is a dance that cherished everyone, and needed everyone to make the dance happen. We could not be spectators, we had to participate, while under the shaded arbor, we prayed and sang and danced with the dancers. Women collected sage, the men helped to build and repair the arbor, cut wood, and the women made the sage wristlets and anklets to protect the dancers. There was so much that was necessary to make the dance happen, including cutting and bringing the central ceremonial tree into the grounds, as well as providing food for the supporters to last for four days, and a huge feast at the end of the dance provided for by the dancers and cooked by their supporters. It was common to feed over 200-1000 people at the end of the four-day dance ceremony.

I had witnessed a practical spiritual tradition with values that were geared to create peace, harmony and loving relationships not only with one another, but with all races and with the Earth. We saw the weather working with the dancers and participants through prayers and through the medicine men who would offer prayers and prayer ties.

A few years later I attended a new Sun Dance, that was just being started by one of the leaders of the first dance I attended. He was under the guidance of a medicine man who brought in a miraculous event for all of us to witness.

On the first day the medicine man set up his altar for the dance, as is traditionally done in all authentic dances. He was a black-tailed deer medicine man, which was part of the altar. In other words it was the animal that spoke to him in communion. As he sang the ancient song of the black-tailed deer, an actual black-tailed deer appeared by running over the ridge opposite from where the altar was, and the deer was dancing in circles and figure eights on the grassy hill above the dance grounds. If that wasn't extraordinary enough, at the base of the hill, two lines of traffic, one coming from the west, and the other from the north, were coming into the dance below the hill where the deer was running in circles. I was overwhelmed in amazement as was everyone else, except the medicine man. This was a confirmation for him that he was setting up the altar correctly and blessing the dance with his medicine.

Another time, the dance was threatened by rain. A Sundance needs the sun in order to feel the light of the Great Spirit. Storm clouds are not a good sign for the dance, and it makes it harder on the dancers, due to the cold rain that can come down on them. Our leader asked us to pray that the rain goes around the dance grounds. We did pray together, and within a few minutes, the clouds separated and made an open hole in the clouds above us. The thunderheads, with swirling winds, came to the edge of the grounds, and then the clouds parted over the dance grounds, but kept going around either side of us. It did not rain where we were. Instead it rained around us. The blue hole in the sky let the sun come through. Eventually the storm passed and we had cloudy skies an hour or two later but no storms and no rain.

Speeches that people gave at the dance during breaks were about their gratitude, showing humility in their dancing for families, relatives in jail, or the sick, and reverence for the Earth and one another. This gratitude was demonstrated every day. I witnessed people making sacrifices for others everywhere. Every dancer was praying for someone else in that dance. They were not there to show off, nor to display their costumes or regalia. This was a dance of reverence and prayer for the entire world. They prayed for all races, for all humanity, individual friends who needed prayers, and for the healing of the Earth.

Along with Sundance, I danced with other indigenous communities from Northern Wisconsin to Brazil. Many were mediumistic traditions, and based on the spirits of the land or the spirits that came from the spirit world to speak to us. It gave me skills and also supported me in the beginning of my practice initially as a massage therapist and later as a medium and intuitive and energy medicine practitioner.

In another ceremony in Northern Wisconsin, that my second husband and I and his sister were invited to, I found myself dancing with Star Woman. She is known in most native tribes, who is the darkness behind the stars. She is the eternal presence that holds stars. We were dancing at night in the Northern Wisconsin woods during the Fall Equinox.

I had not experienced her before, but she came in to the ceremony between me and my sister-in-law with the spirit of my daughter between us. Two years before I had lost my baby in-utero. She had been stillborn. It was a devastating time for me shortly after I was happily married. However my daughter's presence had been with me daily for those two years. She refused to leave, and I felt comforted by her presence, even though I had encouraged her to complete her journey to the other side.

Star Woman came in, and danced with us. During a break, I called the leader over and told him that she was here. He nodded affirmatively, and said, "Just keep dancing with her." So I did, and after several rounds where we would dance around a fire, she said to me, "I am going to leave. Now watch! It will take a while." When she left, I could feel her leave and in a minute or two later, I looked up and a shooting star streaked across the whole dance grounds. Everyone saw it, and I was delighted. Then I noticed she took my daughter's spirit with her back to the other side (known as the Astral world or heaven). While I was glad my daughter's spirit was helped by Star Woman to cross to the other side, I started a whole new grief cycle for my daughter's loss.

Later on, in mediumistic classes that I held, Star Woman came in and since then she has returned many times to talk to people that come once a month to my Mother Earth Meditation gatherings. She has been an amazing teacher. Her work with us on the other side, has to do with guiding people to their new locations after death. She has helped many people learn about the various ways people are guided by the spirits of nature, and by our Source.

Teachings Humanity Already Have

Every Earth-Based Tradition has deep respect for the Earth, and perceives a relationship with the Earth Mother as a primary relationship. Earth-Based traditions teach us to how to live on this planet in a reverent way.

People in Earth-based traditions see the Earth as sacred. Living and loving on the Earth is actually a misnomer because we live within the Earth, within our bodies, which are the Earth and within the breath of the living Mother Earth, part of Divine Mother. While western Christianity sees God above us, Earth-based traditions see all of the Earth and Sky as part of God. The spirit world is real and receives those who have died, and remain with families and friends. This is a common understanding in Earth-based traditions.

In the Lakota tradition, I was taught to live simply and use and reuse what I have. Take only what you need, never waste, and share what you have with others. Leave a gift of tobacco, corn meal, or something that we have harvested, and then returned some of it to the Mother. When we transform from the seed or leaf, to what we offer back to her as eatable food, this offers her thanks. Give thanks and gratitude to others who keep you alive such as the plants, and animals. Everything is alive, rocks, soil, plants, and the living Earth herself.

In Braiding Sweetgrass, by Robin Wall Kimmerer, she describes the guidelines for the "Honorable Harvest" in similar terms. While these guidelines are not written down in her Potawatomi tradition, she summarizes how to regard plants and animals who are seen as beings or persons with homes to return to with their families.

This food returned to the Earth is not just something to eat. It is honoring evolution. Plants and animals were all created before humans, and we are the newest addition to creation on Mother Earth, so those who have been here longer have more wisdom, and are considered our elders (plants and animals) in the Potawatomi tradition.

When I participated in Sundance and other ceremonies, these attitudes were everywhere, and before we took anything from the Earth, whether sage, choke cherries branches or firewood; we had the tools to humble ourselves in honor of the harvest. We spoke to the plant and asked permission. If we got a "yes" intuitively, we could harvest, if we got a "no" we moved on. This was part of every ceremony and every harvest for the ceremonies.

The trees were not just huge plants, they are "tree people" and speak if we come with the right attitude and a humble gift to affirm the sacrifice they give us. The Sundance leader would go out and find a tree to cut for the Sundance. He would go from tree to tree to ask permission and let the tree know what the tree's sacrifice would do for the people. When he got a "yes" he then tied a red flag on it, and days later we would go to that tree as a group.

We offered a ceremony, and then offered some tobacco to give thanks and help the transition from living tree to Sundance tree. The Earth is full of this generosity in every element.

But we as Westerners often ignore or assume that we are the superior species and are entitled to whatever the Earth offers. I find the Native way of honoring the Earth as Mother Earth much richer and more engaging with everything around me, and All-There-Is, as well as a much more humble attitude.

Paramhansa Yogananda teaches the same thing! Live simply with high thinking. It frees you up to enjoy what you have and what you can share. In high thinking, he encourages us to enjoy the qualities of God-Consciousness, which are: joy, peace, love, happiness, calmness, wisdom, sound (chanting), light, and power. He also teaches us how to leave Schoolhouse Earth to become one with God Consciousness.

After my Dad died in 2014, I met Yogananda at Lake Shrine Retreat in Malibu, CA. Yogananda's spirit greeted me in a meditation room at the retreat. For the two days I was there, he was present with me walking all around the Lake Shrine and showed me around the sanctuary. I felt so grateful with his loving presence. That is when I started reading *Autobiography of a Yogi*, his famous book that is still in print after he wrote it in the 1940's. That book changed my life.

At an Umbanda Ceremony I attended after I met him in at Lake Shrine Retreat in Southern California. His spirit came with me to Umbanda, and after I went up to the medium to receive a blessing as part of the ceremony,

I came back and sat with the rest of the attendees. He said to me; "This is a very good tradition, it teaches you how to live and serve on the Earth, but it does not teach you how to leave the Earth as the Schoolhouse to evolve completely into God Consciousness." This had been a prayer I had been praying for many decades: "God, show me how to join you and leave this blessed planet." Today I live with him and the masters every day.

Additional qualities I learned in Native Ways are; gratitude, harmony and surrender, this helps us to stay humble. In addition, I very much appreciate the Native Way of listening to dreams and visions. Sometimes our dreams are not just our mind unraveling in the night, they are messages and visions that we can receive in our sleep to assist us.

In most indigenous communities that I know of or have read about, dreams that serve the community are a primary focus of life direction. Ceremonies often come from dreams or change their format because of dreams.

An example of this is in the Anishinaabe tradition. The Ogitchidaah ceremony, by the Anishinaabe people, is a ceremony for the discovery of the self that is held during the Spring and Fall Equinoxes. The ceremony has been done in Canada since many Anishinaabe people left the U.S., and first came back to the U.S. from Canada in the late 1990's. The ceremony was altered from the older one, because a fourteen-year-old girl had a dream that changed the configuration of the ceremony. Rituals with Native people often evolve in this way, and change from leader to leader because of dreams, visions and intuitive understandings. I danced in the Ogitchidaah Ceremony for four years when it first came back to Northern Wisconsin.

What many people do not understand is that God is speaking to us all the time in different ways. We have just forgotten how to listen, and we have forgotten how to approach the Divine without anyone between Sacred Presence and ourselves. We cannot arrogantly and unconsciously abuse, misuse and trash the Earth, and then expect benevolence. The Indigenous people know how to honor the Earth Mother. They have not forgotten how to honor her.

People like Robin Wall Kimmerer are generous enough to offer her inherited wisdom to us from her tribal people. Many others, like poet Joy

Medicine Wheels - Feathers: Jon Munson design, and second medicine wheel with various direction colors: Yellow-east, white-south, black-west, and red-north. Many wheels have a variety of these same colors, often North is white, and south is black. The colors also represent colors of four races of humans.
All medicine wheel colors are focused on the composition of the Mother Earth in particular regions.

Harjo, who was the U.S. Poet Laureate for the three year in a row, is another indigenous person who honors the Earth and her heritage and shares it with those who can listen.

Respect is key, not to mention awe. Often times, when I am confronted with someone who doesn't believe there is a greater source of consciousness, or a great mystery that we are living within, I ask them to look at the palm of their hand. Then I ask them to open and close it. There are 27 bones, two sets of muscles (intrinsic and extrinsic), three different nerves with 200,000 neurons in one hand alone! Opening and closing it involves the brain, nerves, muscles, and our will to do so. Our hands and bodies were not created by humans nor by science. They evolved over time by overwhelming divine creation! The body is created as we evolve in the womb by divine mystery. The miracle of creation happens so commonly that many people don't see our miraculous bodies.

While I have spoken about mostly Earth-based cultures and spirituality as examples of living in harmony with the Earth, any spiritual tradition can support our own personal relationship with the natural world. Nature is Divine Mother, and we need her to live and grow for our own lives. If you are in a spiritual tradition, see if your congregation can support the Earth, if it is not doing so already. This can be one of many ways to help her.

CHAPTER TEN

More Messages from Divine Mother: On The Earth, Ocean, and our Interactions

Divine Mother: "I have brought you out here into the woods, so that you can hear me better, as where you were living is too full of people for you to hear me clearly, as I have so much to share with you.

"Listen to the quiet; miles from any car traffic. Do you hear the wind in the trees down the valley?"

Robin: "Yes it is very subtle."

Divine Mother: "Yes, it is a wind that is racing down the hills. You cannot hear deer walking as they are resting, the same with the bears, and the snakes, and rodents. There is quiet because there is resting. My body and the creatures that live here naturally know that rest is good, and restorative.

"What I wish to share here, is that the natural cycles of rest, activity, foraging, preparation of food, helps every living creature come into a rhythm with this Earth body. More importantly, with the heart beat of the Mother.

"You have not had time to rest, and part of why I want you to be here is to rest. Let yourself be quiet.

"People in the West, and in the East, have lost touch with the natural rhythms of the Earth. This is part of what has happened with people. Honoring the natural cycles, and following them for your own well-being, is critical in helping move you to a new place in relationship with me (The Mother Earth).

"Last night you watched the movie on Netflix about Geronimo. He fought for fifty years to defend his people and their lands. He was trying to stop the Westerners and the U.S. government from pushing his people off their lands, so it would not destroy his people. Of course he lost in the end, but actually he won. He knew that his people were the ones who had a greater view of the Earth with respect and love for it. He knew that some of this could be lost. But what was most important about that film is how he survived in the desert, by foraging and eating cactus, and other foods that were well known to his people.

"That knowledge has not been entirely lost, but it has diminished a great deal. It will be given back to those who still value the ways of the Native people, and who are Native people to the land that will eventually move people from farming to foraging. The population of the Earth must be reduced, though this is being addressed by a few of those concerned with the environment. Yet, it is a key issue.

"There is nothing truly wrong with farming, however there needs to be a more natural blending of the Earth's needs, without clearing and exposing the Earth's skin. Minimalistic land manipulation is very important. There are new farming practices that are demonstrating this, and it is very good. "No-till" farming is what I am talking about here. The film on Netflix: *Kiss the Ground*, has a very good report on 'no-till' farming and on world wide efforts being made to reduce carbon by covering the soil with plants.

"So there are many people practicing "no-till" farming and coming into greater harmony with my body, the Earth. This is good. Now it becomes key to the environment to move beyond this to enhancing foraging as a plant-based lifestyle and another way to collect food.

"People are eating way too much meat. They do not need so much. The more plants the better for health and well-being. You have seen this in your own diet.

"This is the kind of thing I am wanting people to understand that working with me does not mean people starve, it means people move into harmony and benefit from listening to the land, and have plenty. It does not impact the weather patterns to such a degree as farming does today.

"South of your current home in Santa Cruz, are dozens of fields and dozens of farms. These farms use plastic to prevent "weeds" from growing. It is high production farming. There are also farms that are organic and use more natural methods of farming. This is good!

"Now it is important to see that while one is producing more food, it does not mean the quality is good. And on organic farms attention is paid as to how this farm functions, not as a "kick it out" farm, but in greater harmony with the plants, animals and fields. These farms produce a lot of food of higher quality.

"If everyone went in this direction, the price would drop, and more people would be living in harmony with the land.

OCEAN CARE

Hyroglyphic Sun - Acrylic on canvas

“Now I wish to talk about the oceans. This is critical because the oceans house many creatures that need to live there and only there. As humans dump sewage, plastics, chemicals, and radioactive products into the oceans, it is killing off the coral reefs with temperatures rising in the oceans, and killing off the creatures. It is also harming the composition of the oceans, as the plastic disintegrates, it harms the balance of composition of the waters. Your scientists that are studying what the plastics are doing to the oceans and the life within them has already proved this imbalance. A fundamental change must happen here.

“This should be a unified effort on the part of industrial leaders, leaders of countries, and citizens to clean up the plastic as soon as possible. The more it deteriorates the worse it impacts the planet. While there are some people cleaning it up, it is not a big enough effort. Much more needs to happen.

FRESH WATER

"The same is true with fresh water. Everything should be done to protect fresh waters. It is what your bodies need and creatures of all land-walking varieties, including winged, and land-based animals, freshwater fish, and so on, must have to survive.

"While you all know this, oil pipelines and other ridiculous constructions are and have already occurred around waters that provide nourishment for millions of people not to mention animals of all kinds. While many rivers and streams have been cleaned up to some extent, the industrial functions move towards destruction of the planet instead of constructive use of the elements.

"I wish for you humans to move towards choosing one element and focusing on that to help clear, clean, and purify waters, oceans, land and the air.

"While the land is much better than it used to be, it is not as good as it should be for sustainable functioning on this Earth. You humans must understand that as stewards of the Earth, it means protecting and providing for such creatures, not harming them, using them or killing them.

Mother River - Acrylic on paper

Talking to the River

During a gathering with others who wanted to connect with nature, a group of us walked along a river, and found our spots, and offered tobacco to the River. Each one of us had our own experiences.

When I dropped the tobacco and gave it to Mother River, I felt her speaking to me. She was so beautiful, and loving, as though her spirit was a woman who offered her love willingly to me.

"Hello dear one, what can I do for you?" Mother River said.

"Please help me with this sadness I have," I said. This was before my second divorce, something I did not want to go through again, and here I was with a husband withdrawing to go on his own path far away from me. We loved each other but it was not important to him, as it was to me. I was so sad, and being in the middle of it, I could not see the bigger picture.

She said to me, "Dear one, go with the flow, allow yourself to be guided. It is time to move through this difficult time, and if you allow the flow to take you down, into the river of life, you will find yourself in a better place. Don't worry, all is well and you are cared for no matter what."

This helped me so much. I could feel that my life was to stay where I was, and his was to go back to his home country. It was time to let go.

"Thank you Mother River," I said, "I have heard you speak clearly to me."

The Air from the Mother Earth

Mother Gaia: "The Air is the last element I wish to provide encouragement to clean up. You must do this, you already know how. Moving towards peace and less industrial pollution, means living in an environment where you will be appreciating the cleanness of the air when it has very little pollution in it. People's allergies, respiratory malfunctions—including the spread of viruses when people's immune system is non-functional—all have to do with their environment. It is critical to see this! Bad diets and bad environments that have been damaged by human abuse of the land cause many such diseases that are currently dominant today, including heart disease, diabetes, lung conditions, liver issues, and kidney issues. Cancer comes from chemical poison as well as from emotional disorders. This is a fact, doctors already know this, people already know this, and it is time to change. This starts with each and every one of you, watching your diets, and moving towards more plant-based diets.

"It is also true that people create diseases within their own bodies by ignoring their feelings and stuffing them into the tissues. When people shove feeling away, they are not helping their bodies function as well as they could.

"It is most important to know that you can clear this out of your system, as you focus more on your spirit that is housed within the body. That way you get a better picture of how the body is a temple for your soul, rather than something to abuse with bad food and bad treatment of the body.

"What you do to the Earth, you do to your own bodies. This is what I wish you to understand. Everything that comes out of the body, is meant to help the Earth recycle itself and regenerate. This is how you must begin to think when one plans the making of any products from now into the future. How does it degrade and what does it do to the soil?

"When you hurt the soil, you hurt your soul. Why? Because a part of you knows it is not good for the Mother Earth, and eventually it will harm you too or your children, and grandchildren."

Healing Work and How We Evolve in Consciousness

One of the many things I do in the world is to offer people healing and release of negative aspects of the self. This work has been what I do for over thirty years.

One of my main spiritual guides, WuLan, was a Tibetan Buddhist and has offered me many ways to help people through a process called: Heart Path, which is a guided imagery process. As I have discussed in depth in my books: *Heart Path, Learning To Love Yourself and Listening To Your Guides,* and *Heart Path Handbook, for Therapists and Healers*, this process is based on Buddhist meditation process called 'Bodichitta' or the 'Lightning Path.'

Heart Path brings what is resistant to Divine Light to the outside of the heart chakra. In the Heart Path process, we create a garden in the heart with five aspects; inner child, animal nature, inner feminine [being nature], inner masculine [doing nature], and higher self. These aspects join in the present time self as the inner family inside the heart garden around a campfire.

When we bring a subconscious aspect to the outside of the heart garden that feels separate, or disconnected we can transform it with love. We also release the beliefs that cause separation and the pain and suffering into the campfire.

Forgiveness is the key to releasing the pain and suffering, which includes forgiveness of the self for being involved with a person who was harmful, or forgiveness of the self for causing harm. This aspect can also join the inner family, or grow and dissolve into the rest of the inner family.

What I have discovered over 30 years of practicing this process on myself, and with many, many clients, as well as teaching it to others to share with their clients, that there is an evolutionary process that occurs when people continue to use it on themselves or in sessions. People can shift identity to help themselves heal into their true authentic nature. They can change their identity from the physical body to the soul, or the spirit that they are.

Whatever they identify with, their bodies, their intuitive/feeling, which is the feminine aspect or analytical masculine aspect of their minds, their inner child, animal nature, or observer nature, which is the higher self; as they evolve, they begin to identify with light of the higher self. Eventually, as one identifies more and more with the higher self or the observer nature, and releases more and more pain, suffering fear and anger, and identifies more and more with love rather than fear, the higher self becomes a bridge to the Star Essence or our authentic selves. You could also call this Divine Mother Nature, as it is our eternal expansive Love-based Self.

This is what we are here to do: Evolve to our Authentic Selves. This is our Star Essence, our Divine Nature, and our true God Nature.

What Paramhansa Yogananda has taught us through his most amazing bestseller *Autobiography of a Yogi*, is that what keeps us locked in Schoolhouse Earth, is desire and regret. These aspects are released as we work on ourselves through meditation of his teachings and through Kriya Meditation practice. Heart Path, or Buddhist Teachings such as Bodichitta is another way to dissolve the ego. In Yogananda's Kriya mediation technique he offers a path to release the karma of the past, and clear our spine through the Kriya meditation practice. The reason for this is that the spine holds past karma in small energetic blocks also called vritis in Hindu. According to Yogananda, vritis are actually locked in the spine in different chakras. Many of them are in the lower chakras, which focus on our foundation (first chakra), creativity and sexuality (second chakra), and power (third chakra). There can be vritis in other chakras as well, however most of what I have discovered is that they often are locked in the first three chakras.

This is very significant, because moving through Kriya Yoga, or as in

Heart Path, where we release the egoic aspects that feel separate from the rest of us through fear, anger, or suffering, we are releasing vritis, or those locked up aspects of our unconscious.

In any case, we can be released from this karma, and many additional lifetimes, when we let go of these vritis and come into God Consciousness. However, one thing for sure, is we also need to have devotion to become one with God. We do this through love and as we recognizing our own aspects of God Consciousness. God is Unconditional Love, and as we become more loving, and heal ourselves, we can then serve other aspects of God through many different ways in the world.

Healing Fear with St. Germain
pastel on paper

I am bringing this to your attention, because it is what Divine Mother is here to help us with in Schoolhouse Earth. Here is Mother Gaia, an aspect of Divine Mother, discussing the same topic.

Heart of Divine Light
acrylic on canvas

CHAPTER ELEVEN

The Soil of the Soul
Your Life Purpose on Mother Gaia

Divine Mother Earth (Mother Gaia): "Hello Again Dear Soul, Robin. I am delighted to have this time with you at Ananda Meditation Retreat so you can listen to my clear voice. This sacred ground has been imbued with many people who come for clarity. Now you have experienced the clarity of your being in a way that validates and supports your presence.

"Tonight I wish to discuss and share the purpose for being a person on Mother Earth. My pledge to the Great Divine Mother/Father/God or All-That-Is, is to grow spiritually, personally, and in the direction of Divine desires for the good of all for every person that comes on my soil. Your desires bring about a kind of presence that is one with all beings. While Yogananda gives instructions to let go of desires, your desires are not whimsical desires.These desires are different in they are a part of the deep soul purpose a human comes here to accomplish as part of their gift back to the Universe. These are actually divinely instructed desires.

"These are different than the desires of obsessive sex, money and addiction to material objects, alcohol, or drugs, which Yogananda rightly discourages. What I am speaking of, is surrendering to the higher desire of your soul purpose, which is most often aligned with the Divine and the greater good.

"If I might use you as an example, you began your life wanting to be a great artist. Then you discovered you had a greater purpose than to become famous. Your purpose was to serve others with your greater purpose as an intuitive and medium. You have been developing this in other lives over a great amount of time, and this life is the one where you offer your services to your greater life purpose. Now the gift of art, writing, and your psychic gifts, are here to make your life full of all that you surrendered to, to make the offerings you have made accessible to others.

"Your life today is about making art, writing and offering your gifts, without the help of any man or others around you. And you have the grace to recognize your deepest gifts as great gifts for all. Soon you will be recognized in a way you have not expected in the past, and you will find yourself entirely fulfilled. This is your Divine pathway. You have listened and followed the entire presence of grace in your life to a blissful state both practically and spiritually. There is more to come of your offerings for the good of all beings.

"I wish to share this with those who read this book, because you are an example of what I am wishing to share with others. Even writing this tonight, was an act of surrender for you, as you did not know that you were to come to work on this book, even though you felt the rightness of coming for two nights and three days. You are being one with the Creator, with the Mother Earth, Father Sky, and Star Essence of Divine Mother as Star

Woman. Joy fills you with this alignment. So this is what others can do too.

"Everyone has their own path, but listening to the deepest desires of presence in the world and how one gives that back to humanity, gives you a chance to be in alignment with All-That-Is.

"Now I have allowed, in the last Yuga Cycle[5] (Kali Yuga), humans to

5 Yuga Cycles are described in the book, *The Yugas, Keys to Understanding Our Hidden past, Emerging Energy Age and Enlightened Future*. by Joseph Selbie and David Steinmetz. The cycles are; Satya, Treta, Dwapara, and Kali Yugas. Satya Yuga is focused on Heart and Enlightenment, Tretas focus in the mind, Dwapara is the age of energy, which we are now in, and

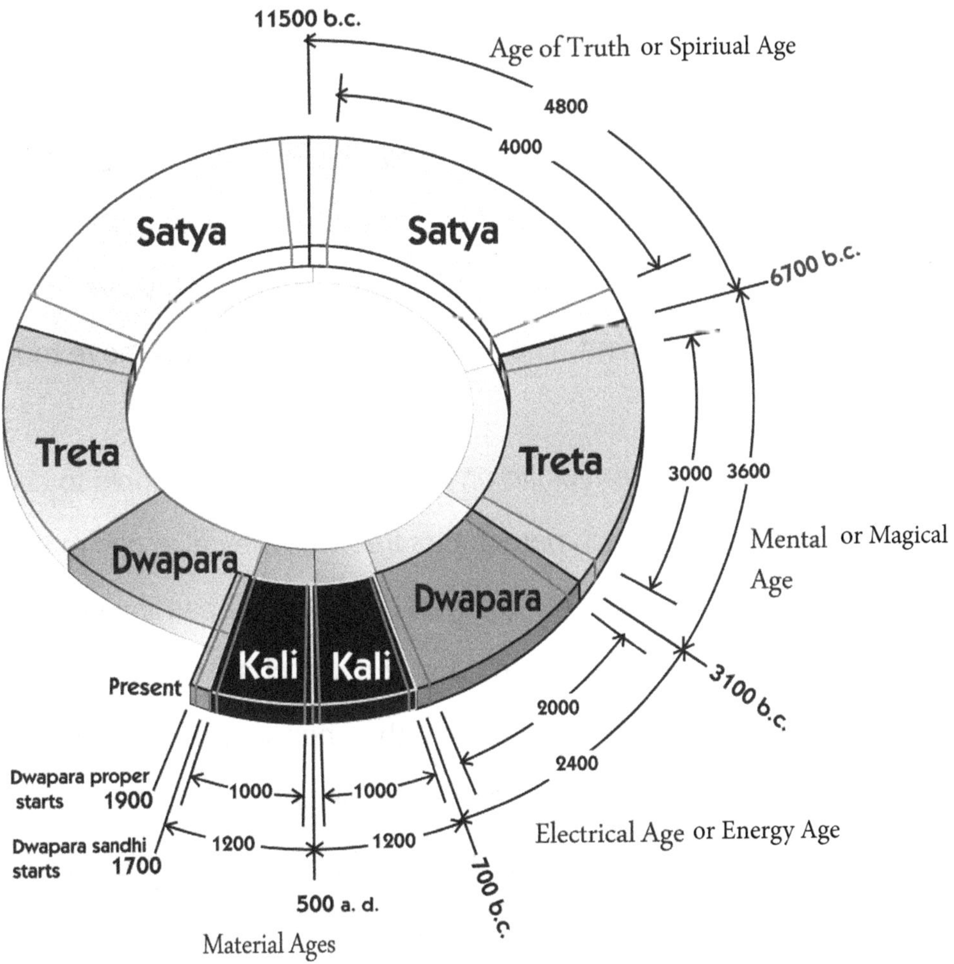

live out their desires, whether of pettiness or of Divine inspiration. People must freely choose to live according to their own path. This is the act of free-will-choice that each person has living on and in my Gaia body.

"The thought that consequences do not arise from the way people choose to live is one error many people make. You choose a path that causes you to have to come back many more times than the Divine recommended initially in your soul growth–intentions set before you were born. Yet here you and others are, as the paths you have followed have taught you hard lessons, and created many more incarnations than was deemed for you to live out.

"The significance of this is that if you follow your heart's desire, or your soul desire, you will feel the oneness in a shorter time frame to live in communion with the Divine, and you will find your way much quicker and more joyfully. You don't have to live through all these 24,000 years of Yuga cycles to reach Enlightenment. The path, if you choose it, will move much more quickly.

"The grand experiment of life on Mother Earth is for people to choose their own path home. For each person has free will, they also can make and choose paths that are not the quickest path home. Learning how the egoic presence gives us hard lessons is part of the challenge. The one who thinks of their self as separate is separate, the ones who feels themselves in communion with the Divine presence are one with All-That-Is.

"As you have grown, Robin Dear, following your heart has become the

Kali Yuga is the materialist cycle which we have just emerged from. Human evolution moves us towards enlightenment.

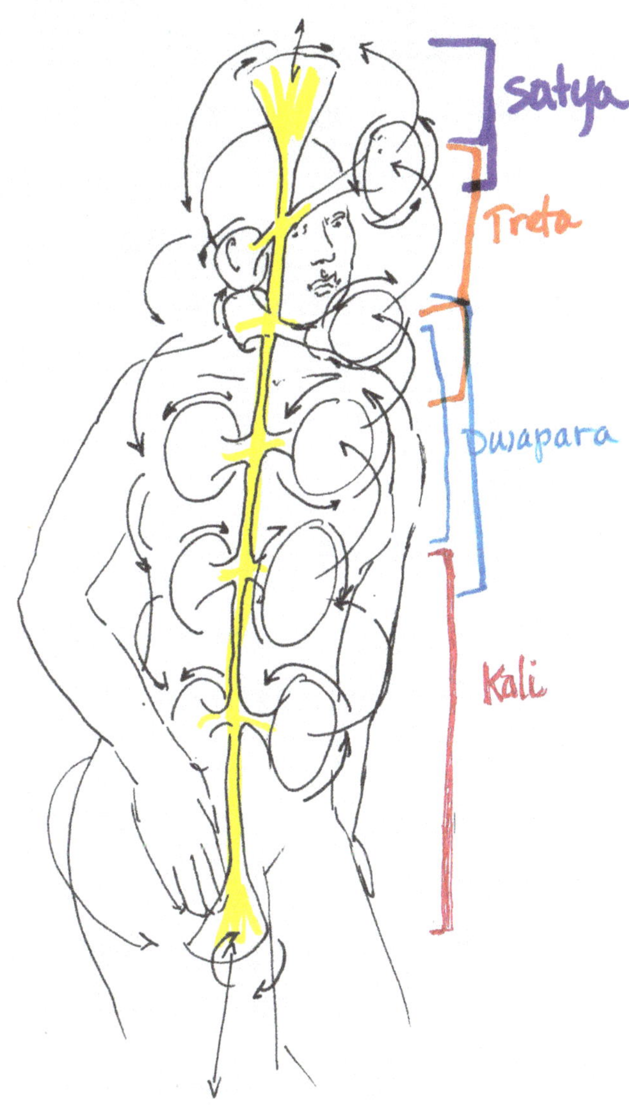

When I took the class on the Yuga cycles from David (Byasa) Steinmetz, I played with the idea of the Yuga cycles as connected with our chakras or energy centers. When I perceive people's blockages they often are in the lower chakras (material reality), and then the enegy changes in the heart (Energy reality), communication (vocal affirmation) and finally in the spiritual eye and crown when the energy is connected with Spirit. So this illustration shows how the Yuga cycles are a part of us - physically, emotionally, mentally and spiritually.

kindling of your deepest heart's desire and the shortening of your need to be on the Mother Earth. So as I use you as an example, others have come to this way too, and you are correct to continue to follow your heart's desire for your soul purpose.The heart's desires are different from the petty desires.

"Everyone must choose Divine Consciousness in their own timing. Some need to live out lesser desires before they can focus on heart's desire. Some need to feel their identity in lesser capacities before they can see that their true identity is with the light of the soul. This shifting of identity is part of the evolution of consciousness.

"So my purpose as the Mother Gaia, is to raise people's purpose towards their heart's desire and meet communion with All-That-Is. My commitment to each person here is to help them move in that direction according to their free will.

"However, when I see people living only to make money, or to indulge in desires that have little or no purpose except to exploit pleasure, pain and suffering of others, it is with this that I say, enough. That is not to say one cannot enjoy themselves and find pleasure in joyfulness. However, there is way too much exploitation of others that is done on this planet at the will of beings that have very poor intentions. Human trafficking is one example, dealing drugs and harming and exploiting children are other examples. Damaging the Earth's soils, air, water, and oceans and setting up destruction, are other examples.

"So this is my message to those who choose to do whatever they want without consideration for others. Their time on this Mother Gaia is limited.

I will not tolerate much more exploiting of others for selfish purposes. This includes corporations that exploit the Earth for their own purposes. They will be destroyed.

"My purpose is to help soul growth ultimately. That is what I wish to do going forward. So those who metaphorically "spit on the Earth" with disregard are not welcome here any longer.

"As you yourself have learned, when one is following their guidance and grace, life unfolds joyfully. When they have negative thoughts and exploit or judge others, their life becomes more challenging. So each human must choose.

"Emotions of fear, hatred, greed, loathing, do not help anyone. Yet they arise from conditioning that has occurred in past and present lifetimes. If a mother or father is fearful, often the child learns that this is the way it is, and unless they examine their conditioning, they have a harder time letting go of fear. The same is true with anger, hated, or loathing as dominate motives. Greed I have already described in previous paragraphs.

"Love as essence is eventually where everyone will go as they evolve. So many people however, choose to live entrenched in fear and anger. This limits their capacity for more love.

"So I wish for humans to learn from this dialog with Mother Gaia. These teachings are true and here for you to shorten your need to come back to the Earth when once you learn that you are love, and love grows as you accept this fact. You have nothing to fear and you may move on to other existences within the Universe once your realize and live this reality. This is Schoolhouse

Earth, a place to grow in consciousness. If you think you are here for any other purpose you are simply wrong.

"One way to begin to learn about love as you, is to love others, love the plants, trees, beings of the Earth, animals, children, sea creatures, love, love, love, and love will be brought back to you. When you love all that is, which is All-That-Is, you come into your state of presence aligned and surrendered to your own Divine consciousness. Remember, you are an expression of the Divine. When you know this in your heart of hearts, and surrender to it, you have become Self-Realized. Wonderful! This is the purpose for being here.

"Your heart grows as you grow in love. Be a splendid person, and you will become a splendid one who grows in Love as Love. Release your fear, judgments, and self-loathing. This is another way to quicken your path. Being present to your core, being present to your path, being present to your needs, and basic survival, all of which helps you come into your own recognition of the Self. Having a teacher is a way one must evolve to eventually. Having an example in the world of a fine teacher is how one may also unfold to higher states of awareness.

"Your love is Divine Love. When you learn from a great teacher such as Yogananda, recognize their capacity to help you, and choose to align with them, your choice will speed you along your path. Everyone needs to find their own teacher, such as Amma, who is Divine Mother embodied, Ananda Moia Ma who was the embodiment of Divine Mother, and Jesus, or Baba Ji Krishna, such as many teachers who are here to help people expand their love capacity, and expand their greater awareness of who they also are.

"The line of Gurus or Teachers in Ananda, and Self-Realization Fellowship, are very strong in their way that truly helps others. When one aligns with them, they give you the opportunity to come into awareness, through their light, waking up in consciousness much faster than fumbling through lifetime after lifetime. It is the Lightning Path, as has been stated by one of your guides, Master WuLan.

"One finds their teacher, when they are ready, and when they ask for one who can help them release their egoic fear-based or anger-based consciousness, then they come into a love-based awareness. This is the true path no matter who teaches it.

"I am sharing this so that people can understand that they are not just here on Mother Earth to have fun. While I am glad to see people enjoying themselves, it is not what you are here to learn from. Learn from life's lessons. Deepen your awareness, by learning from the One-That-Is-Love. You will find this as a part of your love and support pool to help you grow.

"Don't resist life's challenges, stand and face them. Then let yourself move freely toward more love. Don't resist the challenges that life offers you, dive in, as you will find your soul growing and thriving in that new world. Let us continue another time.

"You are loved Robin Dear. You are greatly loved."

Divine Mother Intervenes - Acrylic on canvas

CHAPTER TWELVE

Divine Earth Mother- Forgiveness as Key to Releasing Karma

Divine Mother: "Tonight I want to discuss something that has been an issue for many people that live in this world. That is; toxic relations. When people enter into relationships with a partner or are born into relationships with those who have ill will towards them, it becomes a wounding factor.

"What becomes clear later in life either as a grown child, or more clear with a harmful partner, it is important to realize that there is karma there in the challenges and love. What is karma, but a life-balancing act. So if the karma with others is negative it is because you have been working out a relationship that has had complications in the past and needs to shift and change.

"An example is someone born into an abusive family. Say the father harms the children regularly by hitting or abusing them. What is the relationship of an innocent child to that father? If you take it back in time before the child was born, and before the father was born, you can perceive how someone might need to balance the relationship and where arch enemies often come into family relationships to clear the karma. Enemies in past lives often come in to make peace and clear away the past harmfulness.

"This is not to condone any kind of harm a person might perpetrate on another, especially children. It is to say that once you see the reasons for such a harmful relationship, you see that there is forgiveness necessary between the adult child, and the parent, or the siblings, or partner.

"Forgiveness is how you release karma, not only with the parent or sibling, but with one's self. Self-forgiveness is critical to calling forth the end of a karmic cycle. You can forgive a harmful person if you realize that you have caused harm to them at some point in the past. So forgiving yourself for harming them, and forgiving them for harming you, ends the cycle.

"Some people may not believe in past lives. However, if you think about it, past lives are the only way a person could possibly learn all of the lessons a person has to learn coming into Schoolhouse Earth. This place on my body surface, is the place that makes for life lessons to occur. My intention as Mother Gaia, is to allow cause and effect to play out into the actual reality that one stems from. This is critical to the opening of change and spiritual growth.

"As you grow you become more aware that your higher self, or your divine nature of the soul, is who you are—not your physical body, not your mind—but the heart. Now the physical body does reflect your soul, as does your mind, however they are not your soul, they are reflections of the soul.

"One begins often by identifying with the body first, or their sexuality, male, female, or somewhere in-between, gay, bi-sexual, or someone whose identity is tied up with their physical presence. It is a good place to start, but it is not the ultimate identity.

“Some find their minds the main source of their identity, especially if they are quite bright. What is critical is that the mind is a vehicle and instrument for the soul, not the end all to beat all. Many brilliant people make this mistake. Because so much comes from the mind, such as; which profession you choose, and your expertise in it, or your understanding of things in life, the mind is often credited as being one’s identity. However, it is not.

“Some people also identify with emotions. ‘Emotions,’ as Robin likes to share, ‘are where the rubber hits the road between the body, the mind and the spirit.’

“Sometimes the emotions are what needs to be handled before one can become aware of the life lesson that is needing to be learned. However, emotions are reactions to events that occur. They are not who one is, only the reactions one feels. This is not to say that feelings are not critical to learning about your self as a Divine Being.

“Spiritual growth comes often through sensing. This is good! Feelings are good! Anger sets boundaries when they have been crossed, fear comes when someone threatens another. Hurt comes when someone intentionally or unintentionally steps into a pit of pain you have been burying. This is common. Feelings tell you where you are in your existence. They also lead to experiences that you might have with astral beings that live around you. This is good!

“So what is left to identify with, if not the body, mind, emotions? Well it is the spirit, your light, of course. Your presence, this is wonderful to understand, that this presence that you are, is unchangeable, it can glow brighter, it can learn things, but it is not anything but love, if you are aligned with your true nature as part of the divine expression of love and light and goodness, you have become Self-realized. This is the ultimate goal of life on Earth.

“What comes as a result is; joy, peace, happiness, calmness, and enthusiasm for life itself. Life force that lives through you is your essence. Your soul is connected to that essence, and your soul, your light, is who you are.

“The purpose of sharing this with you humans is to understand where you are in your lives, and where you are in the world. As you grow and change, as you let go of outmoded beliefs such as; “I am not good enough,” or “I can’t do it,” or “I am not strong enough,” then the focus of your life changes and becomes “I deserve to be loved, cherished, and joyful.” This is your natural state: Joy. When you know you are loved, you are also grateful, and gratitude helps you become even more joyful.

“While this sounds simple, it can take lifetime after lifetime of wading through drama to understand how simple life actually is. Love is the key. You are love, and when you align yourself with teachers that can help you get to that love within, then you too become aware of your own sacred presence.

“You are already sacred, but unless you realize it, and realize that others are too, then you cannot come to that as a reality of your existence. When you do though, you become glowing with gratitude and love.

“So my dear souls, know that your life purpose is to come into your

Self-Realization. You are who you are as Divine Beings if you can shift your identity and move from self-love to Self-love. This is a key, loving the self to Self.

“Think of all the phrases that have been taught that are lies: ‘Children should be seen not heard.’ ‘Why do you think you’re so good?’ ‘Who do you think you are?’

“It is time to come into your own light and realize with humility, that you are part of a bigger picture. The life force that lives in you, is part of All-That-Is. Joy comes from love and peace within. It comes from teachers who are in love with life, and let their light shine beyond personalities, beyond quirks, and focus instead on love.

“So beloved humans engage your spiritual path and know that there are those who are here for you and want to help, if you are open. You do have to put effort towards the learning, but the Universe, the Divine, will do most of the work to meet you if you are sincere.

“Be love, and then you will graduate off this Earth, to become one with the force of life that lives you, and you will never perish.

“That is enough for tonight. Love is you Robin.”

Robin: “Blessed be Divine Mother Earth.”

CHAPTER THIRTEEN

Humans and Nature

Divine Mother: “The film you watched the other night “Kiss the Ground” is a wonderful take on humans need to change their way of planting and gardening. Plants absorb carbon, while they release oxygen, while humans, breathe in oxygen and breathe out carbon. The plants absorb carbon and store it in the Earth. This is why carving up the Earth is harmful, because it exposes the very skin of the Earth that has absorbed the carbon, it reverses the cycle of compatibility with humans and plants.

“Humans can no longer work against the Mother Gaia. Work with the natural ways of the Earth or else. What is the *else*? It is clearly death for people who don’t care and just want to make money. It is death for thousands of people, because the Earth cannot have species that do not see that the ways of this Earth have developed over millions of years, and the disruption by humans is not acceptable.

“Period.

“Now what I wish to say to those who are planting and diversifying crops--their planting is wonderful that you have caught on! Everyone needs to proceed in a way that works in alignment with nature. This is critical. Painting pictures that reflect the world as one knows it, making and supporting changes that help the Earth, these are essential ways to help the world. When you help the Earth you help yourselves.

"Your bodies are the Earth. Your bodies are extensions of this Divine Mother. And it is important that you see this. When you shift and make changes the Earth knows. So each person can move forward by helping themselves align with natural processes. The more people—and especially Farmers, that do this—better the alignment with Mother Gaia.

"One thing that farmers need to see is that they are not just holding up a tradition of their families, nor are they just making a living. They are here to work as sacred extensions of the Divine Mother who is one with harmony and peaceful movement towards a sustained future. Recognize that love is the key here, do you care about the Earth? Then make an effort to farm in a way that moves with the Earth, not against her. Don't hesitate to move towards helpful healing.

"The recent volcano that erupted underwater near the South Pacific, is an example of the power of the Earth. I demonstrated this in a remote corner of the Pacific Ocean to release some of my energy towards the disregard by humans. It is a tremendous reality of painfulness for the nearby islanders. As their internet was cut, power lines, and they were cut off from all communication, the way they were just a hundred years ago. However, what is important to know, is that each eruption brings people into a reality check.

"You are not more powerful than nature itself. So realize this.

"So listening to the Mother, and surrender to the alignment of what is good for people. This is most important. See that for yourself. See that for your family and generations to come. This is critical to understand.

"The idea that there is such a thing as 'weeds' is something to take in and realign yourself with – there are no weeds, or useless grains. Everything is useful, each grass blade, each plant, and everything that grows from the Earth, there is a use for them, not just by humans, but by other species.

"Speak to plants, and they will tell you their purpose and what they need. Make a small offering of tobacco, wheat or corn, rice or flour, and know that you cannot separate yourself from them. Once they begin to share what their use is, then you will know how to be with all plants, and enjoy the communion.

"So once you speak to nature, you begin to understand that nature is a teacher. And it will continue to teach, as long as you wish."

01/23/2022 Okay Mother, I am here to serve. What do you wish to share?

Divine Mother: "I want to talk to you about your left arm and why it is congested."

Robin: "Great! Thank you."

Divine Mother: "You will notice that there is a crust or a scab ethereally on the outside, as if it were scraped and has a huge scar on it from your shoulder down to your elbow."

Robin closed her eyes to feel into it.

Robin: "Yes I feel it and perceive it."

Divine Mother: "This came from a past life. The "scab" actually goes up your neck. In a past life you were attacked when you were a woman in another life, it was an invading army. You were Asian, the “army” attached a village that you lived in.”

Robin: “I see I am dressed in white and with a turban on, and a dress that is sleeveless.”

Divine Mother: “Yes. This scar is from a time when you were captive, and they were trying to get information from you. You refused to speak, and they burned you, and tortured you. I want you to see that it is from this lifetime, and you no longer need to carry this scar or the pain.”

Robin: “I feel it from my neck down my arm.”

Divine Mother: “Bring that aspect of yourself, bring her to the front of the heart garden and you can heal her.”

Robin: “Thank you Divine Mother.”

Divine Mother: “My pleasure to help you comes into your radiance: This scar, that you still carry, is holding you back, even now that you are a Golden One.”

Robin: “Did I die with this scar?”

Divine Mother: “Yes, and you were in such shock, that it froze you into that scar and it was for nothing but thievery. The raiding party were stealing land and food, and pushing you and your kin off their land. It was not expected, and it is why you were so in shock. She died thinking that it was so wrong and unnecessary. Yes, it was. Let your shoulder heal now.”

Robin: “I have her in my heart garden. She is releasing the grief.”

Divine Mother: “This is a result of no conflict, there was no karma prior, you were not in conflict, they just invaded, burned down your village, and you were caught inside one of the houses, your house, that burned to the ground."

Robin: "Was my ex-husband one of the invaders?"

Divine Mother: "Yes, he was."

Robin: "So is our karma complete here?"

Divine Mother: "You have forgiven him prior to this, and now you must forgive him for this lifetime too."

Robin: "I forgive him. I forgive myself for being unaware of this invasion. And I have put him in a mirror ball so he can see what he has done to me, and others in the past."

Divine Mother: "Okay, but the mirror ball is more than he can take today. Release him from it, and let him deal with his own karma. His karma is not your problem at all. It is his."

Robin paused and worked within for a few moments.

Robin: "Okay, I have forgiven and released him."

Divine Mother: "Good, now allow your arm to move where it can, and let yourself be one with your golden being."

Robin: "Thank you Divine Mother. I am so grateful."

Divine Mother: "This was important to clear, so you are healed from past lives with a man, and you get your own house back. This process of finding your house is going to be healing for you. It is good, and we will find you a good place."

Robin: "Thank You Divine Mother. I am so grateful."

Divine Mother: "That is all for tonight. You will have lots of other opportunities to talk with me, just let yourself heal at Wilbur Hot Springs tomorrow."

Robin: "Aum, Shanti. Aum. Thank you for this time at Wilbur Hot Springs. I feel so much better and healed."

Divine Mother: "You have done very well. Your time at Wilbur was very good. Your ring is back there at the dressing area. It may not be found by someone other than you. When you go again, you might find it. Otherwise I would let it go. A new ring will become yours soon enough."

Robin: "Okay Mother. Anything you want to share Mother Divine??"

Divine Mother: "You are such a dear one. Robin, your love and generous spirit are truly an extension of Divine Love. Your ability to move through your strife and come into alignment with yourself again is an example to others, and I want you to share this for the benefit of those who are trying to understand healing. This is very important for others to witness in this book. I want you to know that if you cut anything out, it would damage the over arching work of the book. You build to a creshendo of love, and this is wonderful.

"I want you to see that this book will be very important for many with your skills and talents. Each skill you have learned you have earned. This is all good. You need to see what a loving being you are."

Robin: "Thank you Mother."

Divine Mother: "You impact many people, just with your smile."

Robin: "I am so glad, and somewhat embarrassed."

Divine Mother: "That is all for now. You are still on vacation. Relax!"

CHAPTER FOURTEEN

Mother Earth Meditation Group
The Power of Prayer

Since 2004, I have been offering Mother Earth Meditation gatherings once a month. Since the recent pandemic, we have been doing the session both on-line and in-person. This recent channeled session was done on December 21st, 2022 on the Winter Solstice.

Divine Mother: "Hello my Dears, It is Divine Mother. I am here to bring us together, and to recognize how nature helps us evolve, and that is tonight on the Winter Solstice. I wish to say that I am grateful for this group and Robin's channeling so she can bring into this group the reality of Divine Mother to all of you. There are many parts of myself that you may know, Star Woman, Kali, hmm, Black Madonna, Madonna, all the other aspects of the Feminine, who have given birth to this Universe and continue to nurture it.

"And we are at a very critical moment when people must embrace the Earth as part of themselves. The Earth is not just a solid block it is a living being that is here to support, discuss, talk to all of you, and it can help all of you to come into greater connection with your own Divine Consciousness. That is what the Earth is set up to do. And the Mother Earth, is the being that lives in this great, great, planet, and if you think about your own bodies and how you fill them with your light, imagine this great soul, large enough to fill the entire planet. That is Divine Mother, Divine Mother of the Earth, Mother Gaia, that is the aspect of this one, that I am.

"There are spirits in each of the mountains, each of the rivers, each of the valleys, and entities and energies that live in the springs, live in the grasses, in the animals and critters, all of that is, it is important to see this, recognize it, all of that is part of the Divine. It is important to recognize it, because this is the next step for humanity beginning today at Winter Solstice, 2022.

"YES. This new year will be a revelatory year of transformation, of movement further into this new age that we are now in. The East Indians call it the Dwapara Yuga, and it is the beginning of a new time. We are two years into this age, and 2023 is the third year, and the transformation into this age will being in Energy to supplement and support this new age of Energy Medicine, with more psychic abilities with more understanding of your intuitive capabilities, and with the energy of divine consciousness that brings Unconditional Love. This love embraces all creatures and all beings and all of those who are here to speak to harmony, peace, love, and understanding. Today is a very special day; the Winter Solstice so that we understand that this is the direction that humanity is going; that is loving of all things on this planet and this Earth in a better way.

"Do you have questions, comments thoughts? Feel the light coming in. Each of you are an aspect of this Divine Light. It has been embedded in all of you as part of your soul part, of your inner light; that true light is who you truly are."

Michael: "Divine Mother this is Michael: How can we best raise our consciousness to Unconditional Love that you are speaking of, and how do we embody that, and bring it into your consciousness?"

Divine Mother: "As you shift your identity from your physical body, to your emotional body, to your mental body, to your spiritual awareness of your light, that is how you transform in to your Divine Unconditional Love. Most of the last age we have come from was a material time where people identify with their physical bodies rather than their light. They might even identify with their inner child or might identify with their animal nature, consider themselves like a bear, or a mountain lion, or a squirrel, or a crow, those are other identities, and the wisdom of those creatures are truly wise. AND they are not your light essence. Your light, your presence, your divine consciousness, your love, the more you are connected with the unconditionally loving presence of your own being, the more you are identified with your divine nature.

"And there are many ways to get there. Meditation is one of the most effective ways, there are different forms of meditation; The Tibetan Buddhist mediation, called Bodhicitta (awakened or enlightened mind), which is the foundation of Heart Path, is very effective. It is called the 'Lightening Path' in Tibetan Buddhist mediation.

"Yogananda's teachings of Kriya meditation is another very effective way. There are prayers, and meditations in the Christian path. In the Jewish tradition, understanding and questioning things, is how a lot of Jewish people understand God.

The most effective way is to listen to the channel of light through your being, knowing that all beings are part of that light, that light is your life force energy. And it lives in and through everything. It is life itself."

Michael: "The light is not the dark, our fear is not God, our eternal nature is bliss. Yes?"

Divine Mother: "Yes, Life force is God's presence and as you identify with it, it lives through all of you, through everything, every tree, every rock, every ocean, every river, and as a human, you have the ability of coming into Divine Consciousness of Light. You have an awareness of coming into it much better. Where animal nature is instinctual, it is what is born in them as reaction or an action, that is not the life force, that does not mean it is not sacred, but it just means that as you are human you can transcend that animal nature and move into human nature and eventually into your God Nature.

"Feel the light coming through you right now. You may feel the grace like a light filled waterfall coming through and over you. That is Divine Energy flooding you, the light of God, of grace. Each of you have that capability and for you to be present tonight celebrating this day of launching into this New Age, and into this next year is affirming your awareness.

"The irony of the darkest day of the year is that people light candles! They make lights happen around their homes to celebrate this beautiful time. And yes you must go into the dark to bring the light there, to reveal what is hidden so that you can then come up into greater consciousness. So the dark time of the year is a gift to go in within the self, to feel those parts that may be resistant to being in the light.

"Once you see them, once you experience them, you see their fears, anger sadness. You can love them and they can awaken. They can awaken to presences, to present time and present awareness and come into the moment and not live in the past. This is a healing that many of you know that Robin does, and that many people do that can bring you into this moment into this bigger way, instead of a subconscious part of self that is buried in the ground or underneath you. No - you can be with those parts and embrace them.

"When a traumatic event occurs, part of you can break off, especially if you are sensitive, and that part can stay in the trauma and try to figure it out and if it doesn't figure out, it will just spin, spin, spin around in that moment where the trauma happened. Now it stays in your field but it is spinning, it is turning, it is in a whole different awareness, and when you can see it for yourself from your witness self, as your higher self, your observer self, you can see that broken piece, and you can send love to it, and it stops the whirling so it can begin to step into your heart and throw away the old pattern, as you can to understand what happened. It stops the whirling, so it can again step into your heart and throw away that old pattern and understand what happened then. Forgiveness is the key to healing.

"So it is very important to love unconditionally those aspects of yourselves that are fractured, or broken off, or separated so you can heal it. Healing can happen in so many ways. Sometimes it can happen in just having fun. You can dance your way into joy."

Mary Ellen: "Divine Mother, this is Mary Ellen, I would appreciate some guidance on some struggles I have. There is so much suffering that I see every day, with many people, and I have six very good friends that have serious illness and a lot of stress. I would like more insight on how to cope with suffering. Being present with my friends and have good boundaries around them. And just accepting that—this is their story and my life is this way—theirs is that way."

Divine Mother: "Very good question, yes, so when you have people around you that are suffering it is your love and compassion that is helpful, and it is not your job to fix them, they must figure out or recognize the place they are in, and come into the reality of the present moment, and help themselves, or get the help they need in other ways. If you feel drawn to be there and support them, then your karma is to help that person. But if you are aware that there is nothing you can do physically for them or emotionally or mentally, then you can pray for them spiritually. Your prayers can make a huge, huge, difference. If you are not drawn to help them, then it is your prayers that can do the best for your friends.

"Robin had a client that she was concerned about, some very difficult things about her. Robin asked, 'Should I contact her?' The answer was no, and she had come for healing and Robin did a lot of healing and praying for her. The message was: 'Karma, in a pool of karma, not yours to be caught in.' That was a revelation, there are also some family issues, and there was a family issue but it had nothing to do with Robin she was concerned about it and wanting to help. “It is not your Karma, it is theirs.”

“Sometimes you have to recognize your limitations too of what you can do and those limitations are important to notice, and the truth is, as many of your age, move into your 70’s 80’s and even 60’s, the fact is that many people find their path out of this world back into the astral world. And sometimes that path can be challenging.

“When people are not aware, or do not wish to be aware of what their karmic circumstances are, sometimes the suffering they go through is a way to awaken their soul or to heal the karma. Pain in the body is related directly to karma. Burning up the karma is sometimes going through the pain. Now that doesn’t mean they can’t take some kind of medication to ease the pain. But the reality is that karma is burning up in the body as the pain is being lived through. And that can help you step back and recognize your limitation of what you can do for them and what you cannot do for them. So this is very important and a very good question, and of course your kindness, you love and compassion are always helpful and healing for yourself and others.

“And for those, for instance, that are homeless ones on the street, sometimes you can’t always give them money, or feel it is yours to help them but you can always pray for them. Because mental illness in this country has been thrown out on the streets and that is a shameful sorry situation. Also people’s homeless with the high cost of things here for some people, it is where they end up, doesn’t mean they have to stay there, it means they can stop and move forward, and some have given up. And some that have given

Dancing in Star Essence - acrylic on canvas

up, there is nothing you can do for them, except pray for them.

"And your prayers do help. Your prayers are a way for sending energy to others, who have been not willing to look at their deeper issues, and sometimes they are not capable of it. They don't have the strength to do it.

"But you can love them, you can send love to them, and just as you may be bringing a part of yourself before the heart garden that is spinning around, you can bring them to help them stop their spinning in harm or hurtfulness. You can also call on your guides when your friends or relatives are not capable of connecting with their guides.

"You all have guides, you all have angels, every single one of you, and if they or you do not want help, then you can do nothing even the angels cannot do anything.

"When Robin worked in the men and women's prisons, and there was a woman in the women's prison there that she wanted to support with counseling. And the woman was determined to do everything herself. She was homeless, she had been drug addicted, and here she was in jail living out a sentence. Robin said, 'You know you have Guides.' And the woman said, 'Oh, I don't want any help from anyone, I can do this myself.' That was her ego. Her ego demanded that that is what she had to do. She needed help, but she could not see it in herself. Even in that very difficult situation.

"So people can be in their situations because they need to be there, until they are ready to move on or receive help. She was able to receive help from Robin, and if she could have received more help from Robin, Robin would have lifted her to another level. But that did not happen.

"So you have to recognize that everyone has their karmic story that they are living out from many, many, many, lifetimes, not just from this lifetime. And so they are working things out whether they are ill, or in tough situations. There is something they are trying to learn in those situations that they may not have been conscious of prior. So your prayers are sometimes all you can do, and yes other times you can help them physically. They are meant to learn something themselves, that is what they have to do. Does that help you at all Mary Ellen?"

Mary Ellen: "Yes, thank you."

Anna: 'That helps me too."

Divine Mother: "You cannot always say that to everyone. You can be there, and offer support. But you cannot always save everyone. But love, coming to the understanding that you are light, that you are that love, then you feel your energy moving through you to others and this is great grace without any manipulation offering this love to flow through you, to others, is a great gift."

Robin: "The next thing is to speak of the darkness. It seems important to share what that realm is all about. What do you think Divine Mother?"

Divine Mother: "Life does not have to be dark. The darkness is unconsciousness.

"Those parts of us that do not want to admit, or to be seen, that they have made some error, that now needs to be corrected, but that error is not a perfect world. The world is not about perfection. It is about love. Perfection is sometimes mis-engaged as love and it is not love. There is nothing truly perfect except love.

"You see how funny that is? Love is perfect but nothing is perfect in this world when a house is built beautifully. But if you think of your master teachers, and we are very close to Christmas, and if you think of Jesus – he was born in a barn, with animals around in a hay bale because there was no room in the lodge or the hotel. Now that, is not a perfect situation! But Divine Love was right there. It can be brought anywhere. So this is something to understand.

"Perfection is Divine Love; that is the only perfection living in the world. And that love can make things beautiful, and it does not have to be connected to the material world. It can be just love itself.

"Think of the rules of the various governments, right now. Afghanistan has made rules about women not allowed to get an education. That has nothing to do with God, and it has nothing to do with Mohamed. It has to do with domination, and it has to do with control, it has nothing to do with God or Love, it just has to do with the old age of the Kali Yuga cycle, of the material age, of confining women so they cannot express themselves, except in service to men. What if it was reversed, and the rules were about men, and they had to serve women and they couldn't go to school? Can you imagine that reversal? Would that ever happen? NO.

"So what is important to understand, that the governmental rules of restriction are all about control, and it doesn't mean that every government is like that, but some are, and they adopt some lies that they have told themselves about their teacher, which is not true. None of it is true. So what is important to recognize is the limitation that some people want to put on others to control them. And it is a shame and it's none of their business.

"It would be wonderful if there could be a very large ship that could back up to Afghanistan and get all the women off and out who want to go to school to other countries where they could go to school. That would be wonderful.

"So this it is an example of ridiculous regulations, ridiculous challenges and it has nothing to do with God, or Divine Light or Divine Mother, or love of evolution. They are going backwards in evolution. And we are going forward to liberate women and educate them and allow whatever their needs are, to give them the education they need to help the world. That would be a true evolution.

"Yes, there are two things that Robin is going to write about, that I am working with her on now. One is connecting with nature, and the other one is women's liberation.

"Seeing women as equal to men and also capable is very important in evolution. Not to limit anyone into some kind of role, so moving beyond the roles into quality and love and kindness and love of nature and mutual support, that is very different than you, as a man lives in this box, or as a woman lives in that box and you are not allowed to be anything but a man or a woman.

You know in the native traditions, in many native traditions, there are many different ways that a human could be a human, and some can be a man and a woman, some can be a variety, whomever is who they are. There is not a question about it, they just accept them for who they are and what they are to bring. That is a more evolved view point of humans.

More Questions?

Joya: "It seems like a key to evolution is for us humans, is that we each have both feminine and masculine parts of ourselves. It is not common knowledge."

Divine Mother: "Yes, very important, both men and women, have a feminine and masculine sides to them. And sometimes if they are gay, sometimes inside, both can both be feminine or masculine sides—look both female or both male. Sometimes they can be gay have a hetero-sexual relationship inside themselves and still be gay.

There are all these varieties of presence and being that are not confined to roles. People are trying to explore this today and there is nothing wrong with that, it is actually good and it helps them find out more of who they really are.

Joya, "Beyond gender identification—just understanding—I feel the male population is going through this and not as present to evolving on a spiritual level."

Divine Mother: "If you think about the stars, and that each of you as a star, and how you shine and let your light be seen, there are millions of different stars, some are blue, some are red, some are yellow, some are green, they have different colors they have different radiation amounts and different understandings about the Universe around them, and humans are just the same way, each human is a different star. And looking at each person as a star can help you see each person as a star and see their light, and see what their gifts are, and what they bring to the world and how they uniquely bring that into the world. It is a good way to see things, people as stars. You are a star too, a good way to view them.

Three Stars of the Self
acrylic on canvas

“Any other questions or comments?

“Ahh, so when you think about the divine within yourself you can see that it is both/and; both genders, and anything in between, just like there is a Divine Mother and a Divine Father, they work together in union and communion to be in this grand beautiful Universe. And the ideas that many humans have had about power over others, is when it has caused so much destruction and pain. You can see many examples in past history, including if people share the land and share their world, it is much less a challenge to live here, and they are astounded at how important it is to flourish together.

So it can be fluid. The Universe is owned by everyone by God Nature in everyone. Yes.

When Chicago burned down, many decades ago, it had just been this congested city that was full of places for people to live on. And when it burned down, people got together and redesigned the whole city. They designed it, so that the coast along Lake Michigan was a park for everyone. It also became a great place for architecture, and it was experimented with and rebuilt in such good ways. It is understandable that if people can come up with ideas that benefit the whole community, this is an evolutionary way, a much better way.

Well, any other questions or comments? I wish to bring to you blessings, just receive the light that is here and flooding through you, and feel the grace of all possibilities! Knowing that you are that love that beam of light, and the love that is in you is the love that is in the Universe.

Whenever you shine the light on parts that do not wish to be seen, you are helping yourself evolve to a higher consciousness, all you have to do is bring the light in and the light will show you what has to be healed.

So I am blessing all of you, and know that you are receiving healing if you need it, and you send this light to others that need this healing, knowing that they are learning their lessons in the way they need to learn them knowing that each of you have people you can help and those you cannot and those you cannot are those you can pray for. Namaste.

Divine Mother left and the Christ Consciousness, Jesus, came in.

"Live in the star of your essence, It is I, Christ Consciousness, who is here to tell you to know that you are part of this light and as you own it, you own your eternity. And Bless all of you! And thank you for celebrating my birth."

Star Woman Song: One by one the stars are lit, then we see the constellation, one by one the stars are lit then we see the beauty. One by one the stars are lit, then we see the constellation, one by one the stars lit, then we see the beauty.

CHAPTER FIFTEEN

Divine Mother Speaks about Evolution and Levels of Consciousness

"Hello Everyone, it is I, Divine Mother, and I am here to bring in a lot of information tonight for your evolution and your consciousness.

"So we are going to start hmm right off the bat, with understanding that there are different levels of consciousness. Your chakras have different levels of awareness and connection to the Mother Earth, to other people, to your creativity through your sexuality, through your personal power, and then your heart has another level of awareness where you are actually entering into a larger world. A larger world of Love that is a different level of presence. Then of course your communication in your throat, your third eye which is focused on God-Consciousness, your understanding of your intuition and your ability to see and perceive things, this is all very important, and of course your crown chakra which connects to your higher consciousness and your God Consciousness and the thousand petal lotus on each person's head. The thousand petal lotus is like a flower that brings in the sunlight - a lotus flower that has many petals. And when it is a thousand petal lotus that means the person has the focus of light that is coming into the system.

"This is very important to understand. Each of one of these seven levels has to do with different realities. Now below the Earth there are different levels of consciousness that have to do with several things that have nothing to do with your human body, which is living on the surface of the Earth. But inside the Earth there are places where spirits, that have caused and created negative things on the surface of the Earth, go into the Earth and are bound there, until they realize what they have done and come into their consciousness. So for instance a criminal, someone who has done negative energy harmed other people this becomes a straight construction of them going back into the Earth when they leave their bodies, and they have to stay there until they come into their awareness.

"It is the same with suicide, if someone has committed suicide, they are actually giving up life on this planet and they are put into a place that holds them in the Earth until they realize they have thrown away the gift of life.
"When they forgive themselves and forgive the issues that have created the structure that made them choose to leave the planet, then they can be released. But they will not not leave the planet, they have to go into this School House Earth realm again to overcome their restriction, to make other choices. Until they become aware of what they have done, and forgive themselves, they will stay in the Earth."

SuEllen: "Are there guides down there to guide them?"

Divine Mother: "Yes there are guides but only if they ask for them. And only if they are restricted in understanding what they did was not healthy or good for others around them. They harm--for taking their lives actually harms a lot of other people--who love them and want to help them and want to support them. And they choose not to do that, some have mental illness and they have to work through mental illness.

"Another issue is those who produce war, and those who want to be an Emperor, rather than participate in democracy where more people have a say in choices. That creates basically a way that they have people killed or if they have power. That is a power level issue for some people who are really damning others. So they are held in a place like having to go to jail. But the jail is not bars, it is like a cave, that they have to stay in until they recognize what they have done.

"When Robin was in Umbanda, the spirit in the Earth that they would bring up from inside the Earth, it was part of two things, the first was a ceremony where you would connect with the Earth connecting with spirits who are here to help you. The second is a second ceremony where you connect with Divine Love and spirits here to help heal people.

"Pai Buby who was the chief minister in Umbanda, his earth spirit guide came up from the Earth, and that spirit had been someone who created a war back in the Roman times, and was paying his debt by helping this whole community. So his service was to come in and give the community a path that could help them. This was how his earth spirit was releasing his karma. Because he had killed thousand of people, and this was part of his debt payment. So that was interesting to recognize.

"The other parts or people that came up through the mediums, for each individual spirit had done something in their life that was negative, such as prostitution, war army service, whatever. They came up and were serving those on the Earth, and that was part of the service in Umbanda that was very interesting of course to all people. They would heal something in your system.

"Then the next day they would do a different ceremony where you would reach for the light beings and you would go up to a higher level of light. So their service, these are spirits who recognized what they had done and instead of harming others, wanted to help others. That was how they were earning their way out of the center of the Earth.

"Now the reason I am speaking of this is because it is important to recognize that not everybody on the Earth is here to live in God-Consciousness. This is something that is very important to know. Because there are people who think that they have the right to take things from others, to harm others. That is what the FBI is for is to stop those kind of things and stop them from growing and harming others.

"And the reality of this Earth are people who live on different planes or different levels, one stealing from other people on the foundation, others that are sexually abusive that have to do with the second chakra, those that are wanting power over others that is the third chakra. You see they live in a different plane of reality than any of you. This is something very important to recognize and understand because you can run into people who sound like they are good people, but if their reality is taking things, that is what they do.

"And I am saying this because I am going to use Robin as an example. She had identity theft this last week. And had a lot of her savings stolen. I am speaking of this. She has contacted the federal agents and everything she has to do to get the money back.

"But it is important to understand that there are many people who are stealing through the internet and through fake emails and things like that. They can reach thousands of people than they could have fifty years ago. This increases the risks for many people to find ways to stop this stealing what they have.

"We are protecting Robin and we will bring that money back to her and she will be able to continue on for the dreams that she has had and the wishes she has had.

"But that is something important to recognize that there are many different kinds of people all over the planet and they are here to learn life lessons through their actions. So going after people and prosecuting them as she has done with the FBI and with Treasury Department fraud agencies and so on, this will stop this group of people very sophisticed who have done a lot of stealing from others.

"So it is important to recognize that first of all not to take fraudsters seriously. Second of all to recognize that it is good to prosecute these people so that they pay it in this lifetime in this Earth rather to having to go into the center of the Earth to pay for eons.

"And to help others to recognize that this is part of what happens in relationships that some people are in one form of relationship and others are in a different form. And that is what creates a lot of conflict in relationship.

"If you are in the same level or the same consciousness or the same focus that helps. For instance you know Robin is interested in those who are also devotees to Yogananda or have a spiritual tradition that is about meditation. That is her interest which would help her and help the community and help build her community with Ananda. And the reality of that is finding someone, a person who is a good match interested in a relationship. In Ananda, which she is in now, there are those who are learning hard lessons, who have come through a lot of shifts in consciousness.

"A minister that Robin knows began his early life by creating drugs to sell and he was caught and put in jail for three years. There he met a person who was in the jail and talked about Ananda and helped him to grow spiritually. When he got out, he eventually joined Ananda and became a minister and started a community that grew for twenty-five years. He now lives in Palo Alto and teaches children about science and has a completely different life. He went from lower awareness to higher consciousness because of his devotion and willingness to change.

"So that is not true for all of the ministers in Ananda at all. Many of them came in devoted because they care about sharing the teachings, and most of them do. However, in his case that was not the beginning for him and he started in the pits in the bottom and moved up to such amazing service.

"So what is important to understand is that the variety of different levels of consciousness is not just the seven chakras but has even a broader cycle and many, many people move from one place to another and sometimes they go down again and then they go back up again. This is something to be aware of, you can decline and rise, depending on your actions.

"When people get depressed or anxious or full of anxiety and they are working out of fear base they are not always thinking of their higher consciousness, they can't, you see, they are focused on what is negative not on what is positive. If they switch to positive focus, it will help them find their true path.

"When you start seeing your higher consciousness moving forward within yourself, and you get to the place of being in a circle with God-Consciousness with your Gurus, or teachers with the understanding of those teachers that have helped you evolve, that is a place where you don't have to worry about going back down in your consciousness. But even then you can also be vulnerable with those who are criminals. It is something to be aware of not to be afraid of. So this is an experience Robin has had and now she is learning about the aspects of herself that may still be needing to be healed or evolved or grown into a place God Consciousness. She has done what she needs to do and now it will be healed. And so the downside is the loss, and the upside are the lessons.

"We will bring her funds back for her. Because it has been fraudulent. It will also help the federal agents to recognize how many other people are also vulnerable to such things. Any Questions?

"The kitty is having questions."

SuEllen's cat rubs up against Divine Mother. Everyone laughs.

"Yes, Go ahead Michael then we will go to Joy."

Michael: "You are talking about God Consciousness and our higher levels of awareness. How many people percentage wise, are living their full potential in this lifetime?"

Divine Mother: "Well it is growing. But I will say for those who don't grow and change are about 90% of the people. And about less than 5% are those who are interested in obtaining that God-Conscioussness I would say it is more like 1% of people that are actually moving to their highest form.

"And there are a ½ of 1 percent .5 of those who actually will reach God-Consciousness or have reached it.

"But that does not mean that you can't, what it means is that the focus for many people is not about that. It is about living their lives about living their fantasies and what brings them joy, and what they feel is fun.

"Robin has a very good friend, who she loves very much, who is a poet and author, artist and has yet every night she wants to go out dancing and will have drinks and drinks every single night. Robin is aware of her need and her need for the alcohol and also the need for celebrating her life and how she is having fun, but it is not necessarily about spiritual growth. And if she were more involved in what brings her to her God-Consciousness, she would do less drinking, she may still go dancing and that is fine--there is nothing wrong with that--and where do you go dancing? In a bar usually and that isn't to say that having a drink here and there isn't a bad thing, but it doesn't necessary help your consciousness or help you evolve yourself.

"So Robin goes with her once a week or maybe a few times a month. and has a good time, but then that is it. That is all Robin wants to deal with because that is not what Robin needs to work on, she works on herself and helps others and also has books to work on and too many other projects to work on.

"Yes Joy, do you have a question?"

Joy: "These things happen to everybody, I would say it happens to people who consciousnessly are here, or are consciously wasting even more time. Is that for the reason that they have to learn, like in Earth school?"

Divine Mother: "Yes. Yes, this is Schoolhouse Earth. No question. The reason that everyone is here, is to come into their God-Consciousness at some point and that is not something you can just, by chance, do. You have to have the intention or commitment to do your part of the work to move towards your higher consciousness.

"Many people do not have the intention or commitment. So what is important is that this is a very significant thing focus on, and once you get to that God-Consciousness, you are most likely in your last lifetime. You don't have to come back. Now you may want to come back you may want to help others in different ways.

"I will say that those, like this one who is doing this channeling, she has committed her whole life to her God-Consciousness she will not have to come back she will be living in this angelic realm when she leaves this planet.

"So the angelic realm is where you serve others and help others, and you live in full joy and your fully embodying light. That is God-Consciousness where you are fully embodying unconditional love.

"So the opportunity that you are all here, gives you a very unique presence with understanding consciousness and that each of you have the capability of being involved in your own higher awareness. Each of you could choose to be on that path as well or you would not be here. That is something to be aware of for all of you. Some of you have chosen this path of Higher Consciousness.

"Any other questions?"

Joy: "The folks who are into Catholicism or purgatory, these souls or spirits, are they in a cage until they realize just how damaging their actions were or intentions, or they realize that there is another way? This is the dark, and then the light, until they see the light?"

Divine Mother: "Puragtory is an understanding in Catholicism that is before you move to God-Consciousness, you have to be in this puragory area where you have sinned and harmed others and that keeps you locked in that space once you have passed out of your body. That gives people understanding of what it is like to be in the Earth in spacific places that help you understand where you are and what you need to do to come into awareness, you see, in order to evolve or move beyond that plane.

"So yes, and the other thing is the idea of hell, is being in the Earth, or the red light or the fire light on the center of the planet. Well it isn't that bad, to be honest, it is actually loving embrace of the Divine Mother of Mother Earth who is here to hold the people in their low consciousness until they are willing and ready to move forward and grow and grow out of the patterns and the habits that they have been in. That is something that is very different.

"That doesn't mean that you are torched or harmed there, no, no, no, that is not the case. Unless you believe that you deserve that and then you create it for yourself, you see, you create that kind of hellish reality for yourself, but Divine Mother, Mother Earth, I as Divine Mother that connects with Mother Earth is a spirit who is here to hold those beings to be in tight consciousness in order for them to grow. That is what Schoolhouse Earth is about in any case.

"But when you get to the higher level of awareness you become joyful and you actually bring God, and you bring light and joy into the Earth. You see when you get to the point where you bring light into the Earth and bring the light of God-Conscioueness into the Earth what you are really doing is you are helping improve this whole planet by a large number of shifting of awareness.

"This is why we want Robin to do this book tour because she will be going to places that don't deal with this consciousness, it is dealing with history, but the history is actually about the present moment. If you understand the history of your ancestors, what you are really doing, you are helping yourself to understanding more of who you are, when you realize more of who you are, then you become more close to your Christ-Consciousnes or your God-Consciousness.

"So Robin will be bringing not just her history, but all of her books, you see, she has sold her Heart Path books and history books along with the CDs along with giving the CDs away to those who buy books from her, in order to help others. This is the other part of her work that she is sharing, the reason that she does that is that she has a lot of CD's and can let them go. It is one way to let go of the volumes of the numbers that she has. And it is something to give away, but in it is the Heart Path Process, and she gives them away with her history books it offers them something else.

"So she will enjoy it. A nice vacation. And a lot of work but she is good at that.

"You, Joy, will help her at Daughters of Norway and Ananda Palo Alto when she returns from her midwest tour. And that is the reality of the way she is sharing her light.

"So what I wish to share is these various levels of consciousness, something to understand when you meet someone, to understand where they are in their awareness by talking to them or getting to know them, you get to learn where they are. It doesn't matter whether they are focused in Ananda or not, or Jesus Churches or in Catholicism, it doesn't matter where they are. It is good if they are in those churches. They can still be in a lower level of consciousness. This is something to understand.

"Any other questions about different levels of consciousness?

"When you connect with the light of the Mother Earth you are connecting with her God-Consciousness. So you bring light up through your system, whether from the Earth or down from the sky - it's all part of the same God-Consciousness.

"This is something to recognize. Very Important . Different thicknesses or different qualities, it is like the light of a fire not the light of the Sun. But they are both light. Very different light. But they also both represent all of All-There-Is; the light that is around all of us, and everyone. This is important to understand. Any other Questions? So I am going to depart and see who else comes in."

Arch Angel Gabriel

"It is I, Arch Angel Gabriel, I am here to bring in more understanding to bring in the announcement of the New Age, or the new things that are coming into your lives. This next month we are almost at the full moon. It is bringing in a lot of dreams that you have had about what you wish in your life. It will help personalities and things that occur with others who are living out their lives, either positively or negatively. It depends on them.

"For Robin it will be a great month, because she will come into the kinds of connections she has been working towards for her whole life, her connections are about wanting to share the work that has been given to her through WuLan and Divine Mother, and she will be bringing it all in through the books she has written. This is something to understand that her book tour is really about shifting other people's awareness including her friends and family who she will be getting to see and getting to know.

"For each of you there will be new realizations this next month that you will be understanding that your postion you have been given, the work you receive, the work you are willing to do is your destiny and is what you are here to do, whether you are relaxing, or going to Hawaii, or getting a new job, or coming into a new awareness. And that is what I am bringing in to help you understand.

"Any Questions?"

Joy: "I am thinking I don't remember a lot of details when I am sleeping how will we know where our dreams are?"

Arch Angel Gabriel: "So this is not necessarily your sleeping dreams.

You have your desire dreams to move and share in the world. But in order to record your sleeping dreams, there are several things you could do. One is to have a journal and write down the title that you have in your dream, that will help you when you wake up. Some have a recorder and speak into the recorder, and imagine your mind can point to the issues and record it later as writing later.

"That is one way to help you with your dreams.

"What I am speaking of is this: What are your duties for others as you help yourself? Where ever you are positive things that can be evolved in the next month. So if you are here to do something for the Universe and the world stop right now and ask Divine Mother to show you what you are meant to do and what you can do.

"Any other questions?

"So I shall depart now.

"Namaste."

ArchAngel Gabriel departs and WuLan comes in.

WuLan:

"It is I WuLan, I have come in to be with all of you. Hello, Hello, I am coming in to affirm that each of you will find the path that is yours, and in order to do that, you must ask to be shown it, it is not just coming in and dropping on you like a grape and olive. No, you have to ask for it and open to it. You will be reflective of it. I want to say to Robin; it will all be good. And we have all of your backs and your guides that have your protection and awareness.

"I wish to say to Eve, that you need to wear a mask the fulltime that you are in the airport and fulltime that you are on the flight and I would also suggest that you eat Wellness Formula. It helps your immune system and it will help you stay healthier. I wish to say that to you."

Eve: "Thank you so, so much!"

WuLan: "When you are on a trip you are moving into bacteria that you have not been exposed to, so with Wellness Formula and vitamins, and something else you like will help yourself, this will be very helpful.

"Any other Questions?

"Okay, Namaste."

Sun through the
Leaves
acrylic on canvas with
handmade paper

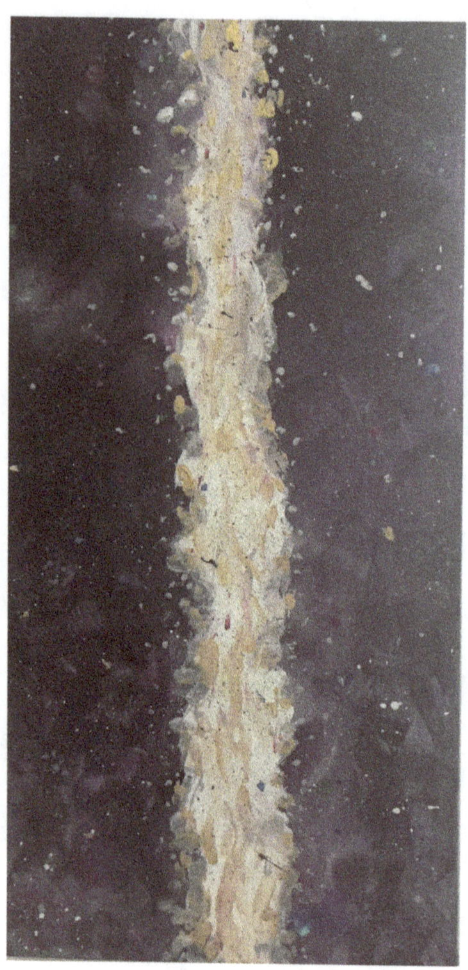

Divine Mother
acrylic on canvas

CHAPTER SIXTEEN

Stories of Challenges and Friends

Robin: "Okay Divine Mother is there a message for me? It seems everything I have tried to do today has quit, or has been stopped. So it seems I am needing to be here in the mountains, even though it is very little functioning with total internet and power outage again!"

Divine Mother: "Yes dear one, you are meant to be here right now. That is the reality. It is also helpful for this book! Think of it this way, the weather has nothing to do with you personally. It has to do with the collective reality. You see the sun is coming out. And hopefully you will be able to go into town a bit later, and stay with your friends Patricia, or Janet.

"For now, be here, you have been given many things by living here. And yes, it is up to you to make new choices. Yes, you have been guided here, and your guidance is good.

"And this dysfunction can turn around in a minute. Be with yourself, the energy of this place, and your love of nature. This will help you."

Robin: "Okay Divine Mother, I am hearing you."

Divine Mother: "Robin, today was a workday for you, doing things you don't like to do, your accounting, and taxes. And you have done well. Now it is time to be with your reality. What can you do? Not much, so BE."

Robin: "Divine Mother, Please speak about the collective."

Divine Mother: "Okay, here is the reality: When people disregard the delicate world balance, the weather indicates that imbalance. Do you see?"

Robin: "Yes."

Divine Mother: "There are people working to get the temperature down and the carbon down, etc. But there needs to be more of a collective connection. This is important. Do you see?"

Robin: "Yes, I do."

Nature Stories with My Friend Barbara Thomas

For many years, since 2001, when I met Barbara Thomas and her husband Jim at a conference in Santa Fe, New Mexico, I have enjoyed our mutual connection to the land and our awareness of the spirits that live on it. Our friendship has been a lot of fun and very wonderful.

I was presenting at the International Conference of Science and Consciousness, and they came to my presentation on 'The Science of Ritual.' There were people there from all over the world. I chose the two of them to present their eldership as Mother Earth and Father Sky.

Barbara and Jim were from Ben Lomond, and I was from Boulder Creek at the time. We were the only ones from Santa Cruz County as far as we knew. We had lunch at the conference and enjoyed talking with each other after my presentation.

When we all returned home they invited me up to their place in Ben

Lomond. They had a guesthouse called Amity Guest Cottage. Up on the top of the mountain, that they called Hilltop, they had an area that was beautiful, grassy, flat and had a labyrinth that Jim had laid out on one side of the area that was surrounded by trees.

I had asked if they wouldn't mind if I had established a sweat lodge up there. Jim and Barbara and I went up upon another visit. They were happy to have it. I had offered it monthly for over ten years, first in Lakota tradition, then an Anishinaabe one, after I had been given the "ladle" by the woman leader of the Ogitchidaah dance.

I also had several workshops in the guest cottage for many years, and enjoyed visiting the land when I would visit. There is also an Amphitheater where there was a clear area in the forest at the bottom of the hill. It is quite large and could hold circles and gatherings as well as a deep place of silence where one could commune with the spirits of the land that lived there. They built an outdoor kitchen and chamber-like chairs that fit the place beautifully.

Jim died about six years after we met. I was divorced in 2008. Barbara and I became closer friends and enjoyed making supper together from time to time.

As we got to know each other better, we had a wonderful time exploring spirituality, as well as talking about the spirits of the land. She was involved in knowing the various guides who lived in the area, and on her property. She, like me could talk with them and acknowledged their support and presence.

She told me many stories about the Gnomes who were around, who wanted to help her as she gardened and took care of her property:

"I had been digging a asparagus bed for two days, I was exhausted I sat on the ground to rest and saw a small gnome about 12 inches tall.

"Standing in front of me he had his hands on his hips, looked straight at me and said, 'You haven't once asked for help!'

"After that I asked for help going up stairs, carrying a suitcase. Once after asking for help walking up a steep stair I saw with my inner eye two gnomes, one at the top of the stairs who tossed a rope to the one behind me. He put the rope around my waist and pushed while the gnome at the top of the stair pulled the rope up. As this happened over and over I named them Yo Ho and Heave Ho."

As artists we shared our work with each other and had an art show together in 2018 at the Mountain Art Center. Many of her pictures had gnomes and spirits in it. She learned about them through many teachers from Scotland, Ireland, and Findhorn where she and Jim spent a great deal of time on several different trips together.

In 2020 her house burned down in Ben Lomond during the CZU Lightning Fires. When she was in her beach place in Capitola less then a mile from where I lived during the covid crisis, I would visit her once a week and share dinner. One time when I arrived, she mentioned that she felt a presence outside her door.

As I tuned into it with her, there was a large Gnome who was in charge of the beach in Capitola. We talked with him, and he said he wanted to connect because he knew that we both could see spirits of nature. His name is Den Do, and we acknoledged him and it also helped to connect with nature around us.

Today, Barbara is ninety-six and moved back on to her property in 2022. The other cottages, including the Amity Guest Cottage, The Forest house, and another small cottage, her studio and garage were not burned down. However, the rest of her land and around the area had been burned by the fires, as the trees show their burn marks all the way down hill to the amphitheater area. Many madrones died from their roots being burned up, and some are still standing, as many have fallen down in the heavy rains we have had in the last few months. Living in the woods is an adventure, as the trees lose limbs randomly, and help us turn branches into firewood.

When the condo I was renting was sold in 2022 after seven years living in it, Barbara invited me to move to Ben Lomond and live in her guest cottage on the mountain. I have been renting it since August of 2022 and she is back on the land in her new home, which is a huge adjustment for her as well as for me. She called her old home, Amity Cottage. Her rebuilt home is called Amity Lodge.

I hadn't lived in the mountains since 2003, and while I love it up here, especially the silence in the depth of the trees, and I enjoy being with wild creatures I saw a bobcat run out of the storage shed yesterday, I hadn't been so close to nature for sometime. There were things I needed to do to get the guest cottage transitioned into my more livable home. However today, I am sitting by the fire and writing, while listening to classical music which is a lovely life.

Recently Barbara and I went to a book signing by an author who was presenting about spirits of the Earth at the Capitola Library. It is a book called; *Sacred Spirits of Gaia* by Camilla Blossom. When I was there, the author offered several experiences through drumming and singing, and she invited Gnomes and other entities such as Mermaids and Mermen to come in our circle on a spiritual level.

When the Gnomes came in, I felt the Gnome say, "I can help you with your screenplay!" I was surprised and a bit shocked that they knew my first novel inspired a screenplay! But as I thought about it, I decided it would be so helpful for them to help me, as I have nothing to do with Hollywood! We shall see what happens!

Barbara Thomas is so connected to this land, and the beings on it. She said to me recently, "The Spirits of this land called you back here." I know she is right. I feel very connected to it. The trees as witnesses that stand around, and I have gotten much closer to Divine Mother. In fact, I feel the stars of my own being living in me now. I also have more time, besides my healing practice, to write this book and make new paintings!

Robin Lysne and
Barbara Thomas
Art Show poster for
Santa Cruz Mountain
Art Center in 2018

CHAPTER SEVENTEEN

Heart Path Helps Us Come Into Star Essence or Our Authentic Self

In this section, I want to share what I have learned about healing work on a personal level. I have been encouraged to do this by Divine Mother to share this with you.

As we heal ourselves, our vritis, as called in the Hindu tradition, or wounds and limits, those beliefs and limits that are stuck in our spine from past lives or from this life, eventually release, and we open into much more energy and to our higher aspects of the self. This is very important because when we let go of trash in our beings, we open to our authentic nature. This is the focus of Energy Medicine, at least in my practice with the Heart Path Process that WuLan, a Tibetian Buddhist Master Spirit Guide, taught me.

Over the years, I have witnessed many people who, after releasing layer after layer of the pain and suffering from the past in the work we do together, they open up to their higher self, and to their star essence. This is the shift from fear-based mind, to love-based heart.

The Star Essence is Divine Mother, or the eternal presence of our Divine consciousness. It is unconditional love. My experience has evolved too into this awareness. When I focus on my own presence, I feel the star presence shining or falling through me as light of God. This Star Essence began to come after other major shifts in my awareness. In the center along my spine, I feel the light of my being flowing and shining all the time.

I felt my mind drop out many years ago. Instead of having my mind running everything, I let go of enough of my past that the mind control let go, and I felt more present than ever before. It began to happen spontaneously.

When I was in the process of my mind dropping control of my being, two teachers of my past, one from Brazil, and one from Michigan, called me on my phone. In the middle of the process I was in when my mind dropped out, I felt like I was in a bubble of fear, and they each separately said to me, "You are fine, let go, just know you are loved." After the second call, I sat down and began to meditate and then BOOM, the control by my mind dropped out. I felt everything around me was miraculous. The sun coming through the branches, the tiny insects, and butterflies all were amazing to me. That was the shift I made, and it was the main opening that allowed my life to blossom even more into connecting with All-That-Is.

Over the years, I have learned to stop, meditate, and feel the joy of presence in love all around me. Now that I am up in the mountains, living among the trees, I feel the joy of life every moment. It is wonderful to be here.

What I know is that when we work on ourselves to let go of our fear and anxiety, we come into our authentic natures. Our higher selves become a bridge to our Star Essence. This is something to perceive in the heart garden. As we bring our higher selves into our hearts, it holds the blueprint for our lives that takes us on the path of unconditional love. This is a miraculous way to feel our being opening up.

When enough of the past is released, our star essence comes in spontaneously. When others are ready to bring it in, I ask them to bring the star essence all the way to their feet, and they are moved into an open, loving presence.

So you can do this too, and when you bring your light within, through your spine, it guides you and you are living out what you need to do on Mother Earth.

The other important reality is that while you can bring in your star essence, it does not mean you are free of all vritis or old non-useful beliefs that block you. There is still inner work to do as long as we are here.

Recently, I experienced another release of a past weeping inner child, holding onto a belief that "no one is there for me." This came about when I was just sixteen months old, and witnessed my mother having a breakdown with hysterical blindness during a pregnancy with her last daughter she was carrying. She was seven months pregnant, and could not see visually, due to all the stress she was dealing with. She was already the mother of four children, and at that time, relatives were visiting from Chicago and became sick with the flu. My Dad came home for lunch and took her to the hospital, and called a baby sitter for me. She stayed in the hospital until she delivered my younger sister two months later. When she came home, she was focused on the new baby. I had disappeared in her attention.

Over the years, this limited belief played out with partners who loved me for awhile and then left, and the reality of being alone for years was in part this feeling of being abandon over and over in different forms.

When I brought my sixteen month old into my heart garden (I did this, at first, years ago but now she needed more help), I gave her to Divine Mother, and Jesus, and Paramhansa Yogananda, and asked them to love her please. They did. Eventually she released this belief, of "no one is there for me" and I felt in my adult-self that I was loved and cared for by Divine Mother, and Jesus, and Yogananda and by those in my life around me.

When she left and went into higher realms after several days of holding her with them in my heart, she released and went back to the astral plane, and into the light of All-That-Is. She was freed and so was I. Now I feel the star essence in my presence, and feel grateful for it. It has been years of working on the unnecessary beliefs and fears. And now I am grateful to live with my teachers within my heart.

As we stand in our Star Essence, and Higher Self, we are bringing in more light for the world. This will change consciousness with others including those who may not be aware of who they are or what they are here for. Prayers can help them heal, and also our desire to make their world better, helps them if they receive the energy of love. As we align ourselves with Divine Mother, and great teachers everywhere, no matter their religious orientation, we help the world, along with the love that we share.

It is my wish for you that you work on yourself and come into your own Star Essence. Aum, Shanti, Shanti, Aum.

Star Woman

So this is what I, Star Woman, want to offer you. As you love yourself, and learn to identify with love as your being, not only as your way of operating, then you will be realized. You will be that which you seek. There is not the other side, there is only this one existence.

What we have in the Earth reality, is what we are speaking of, that 'as above so below.' All are aspects of God. Here is God mowing the lawn, God with his child, God nursing her child. All are aspects of the Divine. The over soul is your Divine nature. You have already read this; as it is in this book that Robin has been writing.

I come to you in the form of Star Woman, but I am neither a woman nor a Star Man, all are manifestations in Nature and in your mind to accept this energy of the Divine. Be with this, be with that: Star Man and the Blue Thunder Spirit are all part of the Divine manifested in different forms.

That is why you can be in the Earth as bear and be also a spirit of the stars. This is why you can be a woman and a child at the same moment. You can be a woman, a child, a man, all are one in the Heart, all are one in the light of All-That-Is.

More and more, you will identify with this light as you, and you will experience this shift. It is coming, and then you will go out in the world and your work will be electric.

The Three Stars (Star One: 6th and/or 7th chakras, Star Two: 4th or Heart chakra, and Star Three: 2nd chakra) are offered to humanity to help in the challenges of moving in the world with their sense of essence, their senses of connection to the Divine intact as star essence. The Three Stars offers a way, a new way, to begin the process of connecting with your Divinity. If you do not connect with it at all, it is an indication that you have a great deal to learn about who you really are. Your essence can lead to the identity with the Divine. The Three Stars leads you to this. But it can also become egoic. "I am connecting with a higher source than you are…." That is not what we are doing here. Each person has their Three Stars, and each Star Being is different. This is what it is that you are doing; identifying with your sameness and your uniqueness at the same time.

All have stars, and all are unique. This is the essence of your being and movement for your being to your Divine Self. It is an identity shift and it is a break through at the same time.

Question for the Divine Presences

Robin: "How is Christ Consciousness and the Medicine Buddha connected?"

Arch Angel Ariel: "Divine Love heals all things. Medicine Buddha is all about healing and is Blue, like Krishna is Blue. Blue represents healing energy. Divine Unconditional Love is the one for you to focus on, whether it is Christ Consciousness through Krishna, or through Christ /Jesus and through Buddha. This is what focuses in the Blue color, or healing essence.

Now Buddha, Medicine Buddha, serves a different population. And Krishna is of service to many other people, so they are all very important. And tied to God and Love, and so being with your Self, helps you see your service purpose and your teachers."

Robin: "Thank You Arch Angel Ariel."

WuLan, "Well, Hello! It is I, WuLan, It is a great pleasure to be with all of you. As most of you I am the one who brought this to Robin along with Divine Mother, and this group and opportunity to get in a circle and be with everyone. It is wonderful to see all of you again and be in SuEllen's home. How wonderful to see you. All the friends that are here and on-line.

"I want to share with you that we are entering into this new time, and we are in a state of transformation. Every month will be an opportunity to move into deeper and higher understanding in this year (2023). This has not been exactly clarified, but I am bringing it in tonight so you are all aware. So if things occur for you to move into transformation, events that will change things; such as celebrations of your children or grandchildren, or a trip you are taking, it could be an opportunity to meet new people. However it unfolds for you.

"For this one, (Robin) we are moving her into screenwriting, and I am bringing this in because it is very important for her to hear. Ha, Ha, Ha.

"Her novels have the opportunity for people to understand their spiritual evolution and development. And this is what it is about under the story—it is about transformation, how someone goes from disaster to a great contributor and an opportunity. These first two novels are about her great, great, great-grandmother. She is just doing another one that she is editing now and about her next great, great-grandmother, the civil war and people who came to this country and how this unfolded for her great, great-grandmother. This is all a part of the next part of her work. Not just writing novels but writing screenplays for the novels. So this is a part of the work she is doing along with a new book on Divine Mother. Divine Mother asked her to write this, and she has been working on this for a long time, and now these books are coming to a circle of closure, and that, her writing, in addition to her clients and those people that she sees, is going to be a part of her life.

"So as her guide, as one of her guides, and her companion in teaching, I would not say I am her teacher, I am her companion in teaching, because she is a soul of wisdom in and of herself. So, we are companions in this lifetime.

"Now what I want you all to understand is this year will be very different by the end of the year 2023. And that does not mean anything negative but that it is moving towards higher awareness and how you can move yourselves into higher awareness. This is very important.

"I also wish to share that: When you are connecting with nature, you are connecting with Divine Mother, no matter how you have connected; through every plant, every flower, every tree, every rock, everything has life force in it. And Life Force is Divine Mother and Divine Friend. Glad in itself is actually the energy that comes through your system and it is the life force that you have and it is not male or female it is actually both and, all the energies of life. That is very important to know. So recognizing Divine Mother balances out the patriarchal focus on masculine nature, the actual reality is all part of the divine flow. This is what I wish for everyone to understand.
Any more questions, comments or thoughts?"

Joya: “Certainly I have had one on my mind. The big question that is how, as Baba Ram Dass says: love everyone. And there is so much chaos, so much negativity and so much ego, so much shooting, people doing things that seem so crazy. I understand the concept of why that is, and no matter what is going on is to put out love. It is difficult and so difficult to put that into different situations.”

WuLan: “Well, if you can see the light in each person, no matter who they are or how they are functioning, this helps to pray for their souls, then pray for their souls. Their actions, yes their actions can harm others, no question about it.

“But the majority of people, if you think about it in this world, the majority wants to be in peace and harmony. Most people are caring and polite, they are not here to harm anyone. So it is a very small percentage however they make the news and then it feels like the whole world is in chaos. And actually the world is in more peace than it has been for many decades. It is very different than World War I or II, we are not in that era any more. Yes there is war going on, and yes an earthquake recently in Turkey, and tragedies 33,000 people (60,000) that died in this earthquake. So a lot of people have been harmed. And when you think of the world as a whole there are millions and millions that have been in peace in a better way. There are wars in Africa, and South America, and there are leaders where they are not considered to be for the people, but for themselves. That has been going on for a long time. And people are waking up to see that they are needing to have a peaceful life, and emigration and all of the challenges of that, and people in countries like Argentina and Peru, South America and Central America have been in crisis for over twenty-five years or more, and Mexico has areas that are harmful and difficult especially near the boarder.

"But the focus on the news media is often on the negative. There are a few stations now that are integrating more positive news. However, if you can allow yourself to see the light in every being, this is how you can pray for them no matter who they are, what they are, or what they have done.

"So this is very important, to align yourself to what is true and what can you do to help the families that have been through shootings as well as difficulty. Prayers help a great deal.

"Robin has a niece that lives in Lansing, Michigan, and her son was working across the street from the shootings that happened at the University, on Monday (Febuary 13, 2023). Her son was put into isolation, thank God, by the police until they arrested the man who shot other students. And her family knew students that were killed and injured. So one of his best friends was shot twice in the chest, he is in the hospital right now and so this is not far, far away, yes it is in Michigan, but it is connected to Robin's family and these things can definitely impact the friends and family and others all around. Praying for those souls can help things a lot and change things.

"There is a huge need for mental health in this country, the need for this has been pretty much ignored. There is only less than one percent of people that the government helps to pay for mental health to help poor people. They know there are 10% whether rich or poor, but the government only allows 1% to be helped. There are a lot of things that could happen differently.

"Put one cost of a military ship into mental health. That is a very small part of the military budget, the people know about this in the government.

"There is a portion of people that are going through mental health. We have gone through covid and the students need help with other people in many ways. We are not there yet. But we will be there if people start to see this. It is not only eliminating unnecessary guns, it is people that need mental health help as well.

Divine Mother and Mother Mary

Divine Mother: "Hello, it Is I Divine Mother. Feel the beauty that we are all living in with this view of mountains, and hearing the turkeys out there in the field.

"We are closing this book with a most recent talk that I have offered to the group that meets once a month. We are focused on how to live in peace and know what is needed in this world to help the future generations.

"The first is to recognize that children today are needed to help convert the destruction of the Earth into harmony, by honoring and respecting the Earth Mother. Teaching children how to honor the Mother Earth is something we can all do. Listening to what you are being encouraged to do for the good of others, is very important. Whatever you use or do, makes a difference for future generations.

"Expanding wisdom and knowledge is one way to help, but then there is another way, to love and connect with the Earth. Connect with the plants, and the wonderful trees and rocks around your home. Connect with those beings who are here to support these plants and trees.

"Pay attention to what is of true value. These values are not material; they are within the soul. Love, peace, harmony, calmness, light, joy, power to choose your path, caring for others, wisdom, and all the aspects of God Nature that Robin's teacher Yogananda discusses, are what is most important. Providing these traits in a home that works for others, this is the importance for future generations.

"I will share what is about these qualities:

"Knowing that peace is not denial of what has occurred. It is working through issues and making peace after the working through conflict. Conflict is a difference of view points and a difference of values. Understanding others views can help make peace. Getting to know the issues and working them out together makes things better for everyone.

"I wish you to see that you are loved, and that love is what you are here to align with.

"Harmony allows there to be a loving presence.

"Calmness allows observation of the situation, and it does not implement judgment that can harm the situation.

"Light comes into the being through God Nature, whether a man, woman or bi-sexual being. Light expresses your highest, happiest presence.

"Joy is what makes life fun, and when you know you are one with Divine Light, you are one with the love of Nature too. Joy of being gives you joy each moment.

"Power helps you to chose the right path, and align yourself with the power of nature. Witness the power of nature as part of who you are. This makes a harmonizing reality rather than a far off distant thing that belongs to others. You have the power of choice in every decision. This makes choices part of your powerful path. Recognizing yourself and what you have done in the world, what you have accomplished, makes your choices aligned with what you are being guided to do. Your strength and power make you choose what works for All-That-Is.

"Wisdom gives others depth of understanding. Welcome who you are as a wise soul. You do not need to randomly offer confusion or ½ truths. Wisdom comes from bringing ideas into your heart to see how it aligns with love.

"Love is the wisest source of being. Then expressing what is true, not what is made up or important for someone's random desire for power over others.

"This is an aspect of self to develop. Your light develops through wise choices. Schoolhouse Earth is a place to develop wisdom. That is what I wish to share."

Robin: "The next spirit came in as a surprise for the first time to share her love and wisdom."

Mother Mary: "As the Mother of Jesus, and as a witness to his death and resurrection, I find it wonderful that 2023 years later we are in a place where people still honor his life. He was an example to us all of what we can all move towards.

"I am appreciative of your gathering and knowledge that you are here to ake in God's light. Your light moves into you through your spine, and now you can move it out into the world by sharing your light with others.

"Love is what matters, and knowing that the soul of us all is one light gives us hope, joy, peace, harmony, power, love, calmness, wisdom, gives humanity what is needed for future generations.

I am grateful to be here, and speak to you directly. Blessings to all of you."

The group: "Thank you Mother Mary."

Divine Mother: "So I wish to also share that when Mother Mary came in, this portrait Robin did afterwards, gives others an understanding of who she is and how your own ultimate option - to bring your light to the ground - that the ground is God-Conscioueiss as well as the sky. That is why the hands of God is there underneath her feet. This portrait shows us how to bring in our own light and let the light come up."

Mother Mary - Acylic on canvas

CHAPTER EIGHTEEN

Divine Mother's Vision of The Future

Divine Mother: "The circle of life is the new foundation of the future. This is what humanity needs to see instead of the pyramid of patriarchy. What works better for everyone, women, children and all races is to see that everyone has a part in the world that all beings can participate in. Not by someone else's dictation, but through their own inner guidance of the light that they are. This is the path of the future.

"Showing gratitude for life itself, with the Mother Earth, Father Sky, and amazing love that comes into each and every person, this is critical for all of life to form into a higher awareness. God is Love, Mother God, Father God and all the aspects of divine presences are Love.

"Be with this, your own divine presence. And it will help you to center yourself instead of being one with the outer world that is not where you are, but with the presence of your own divine being relating to your inner self rather than you seeking solutions to your life outside yourself. When you help your inner world, you also help the outer world as a reflection of who you are inside.

"When you are feeling joy inside yourself without exterior activity, you are feeling the presence of Divine Love. When you feel love flowing through you, that is your God nature. When you bring that Divine Nature into the world, you are bringing the presence of love into the world and it helps you move yourself into alignment with the Creator with everything all around you. That is making this place heaven on Earth.

"The paradox is that this Earth is Heaven itself if you choose to live in love. If you choose to live in fear, anger, sadness, rage, this is bringing hell to the Mother Earth. I do hold those who have done terrible things to others, and will not release them from my inner presence, until they realize what they have done, then they must forgive themselves and their "enemies."

"The truth is all of you are not enemies, but part of the same fabric. Those who choose to murder others or harm them with the intention of powering over the others, this is wrong, it is not what you need to feel or see. So those who have done great harm to others are captives within me. They have lost their free will. This is not to say the Earth is hell, it is to say that for those who do not want to partake in any self-reflection, they are choosing a more hell-like presence, and choose to find their path locked in the rock, rather than in the flow of light.

"Now this is what has been called hell, but today it is not hell. The inside of the Earth also has lovely creative presences that are part of God. Robin's sacred sweat lodge Spirit, was one example of this. He was a lovely guide and such a dear soul who helped the lodge be run correctly. He is a big soul—one who makes the thrusting of power invalid. That is unless you are wanting to meet your guides—and Robin has focused on what they guide her to do. Their guidance with her helps her on a faster path as it resonates with her inner self.

She followed her sacred lodge leader's guidance. He lives inside the Earth, and he is here to clear energies that are no longer necessary. So are the Gnomes, the Fairies of the rivers, lakes and ports. Just feel them, and they will assist you.

"So to align with the Earth, gives you a start to your life lessons. This is very important! So be with your love, and that is All-That-Is. Really, know that you are capable of living in Heaven here on Earth, anywhere that you are. Choose love, and be with your light, your love, your joy, and all will be well."

Divine Grace
acrylic on canvas

Robin H. Lysne, M.A., M.F.A., Ph.D.

As a medium, intuitive and psychic, Robin Lysne has been working with people with challenges for over thirty-five years. She started as a massage therapist and moved into mediumship after 1998.

Her work helps a variety of people from those with losses, to those with inner conflicts that need to be resolved and can be helped through shifting fear-base to love-base, and self-love to Self-Love.

Since 2004, she channels Divine Guides, including: Divine Mother, Star Woman, WuLan (Tibetian Buddhist Master Teacher), Archangel Gabriel, Michael, Arial, Mother Mary, Jesus, and others who are here to help humanity. She offers Mother Earth Mediation once a month open to anyone who wants to come on-line or in-person. New participants are always welcome.

She is the author of eleven books; two poetry, five non-fiction, two novels and a narrative non-fiction, *Kisti's Royal Garden*.

Recently she has launching a "Legendary Women Ancestor Series," with three books of historical fiction and a narrative non-fiction book that brings to life the courage and wisdom of her Norwegian women ancestors.

Her previous books are: *Ceremonies from the Heart, for Children, Adults and the Earth, Mosaic: New and Collected Poems, Poems for the Lost Deer,*

Heart Path, Heart Path Handbook, which contains some of her drawings and paintings, as well as poems. (all published by BlueBoneBooks, Santa Cruz, CA)

Earlier works are: *Sacred Living, Dancing Up the Moon*, (Conari Press). Her poems have been published in: *Fog and Light, North American Review, Catamaran, Porcupine Literary Arts Magazine, Monterey Bay Poetry Review, Rattle, Phren-z online Magazine, Porter Gulch Review, Samizdat, Awakening Consciousness Magazine*, and others.

She is a member of: Poetry San Jose, Poetry Santa Cruz, and the Emerald Street Poets group for critiques in Santa Cruz, Daughters of Norway, The Santa Cruz Art League and member of the Mountain Art Center in Ben Lomond.

Her websites are: www.thecenterforthesoul.com, www.RobinLysne.com and www.bluebonebooks.com. On her days not writing, she sees clients, paints, dances, and enjoys her friends.

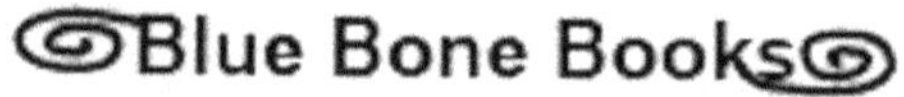

Blue Bone Books Publications:

Narrative Non-Fiction
Kisti's Royal Garden

Novels
The Legend of Randine: Entering the Sisterhood
The Legend of Randine: The Laerdal Letters

Poetry
Mosaic: New and Collected Poems
Poems for the Lost Deer

Non-Fiction
Ceremonies from the Heart, for Children, Adults and the Earth,
Heart Path, Learning to Love Yourself and
Listening to Your Guides
Heart Path Handbook, for Therapists and Healers
all published by Blue Bone Books, Santa Cruz, CA

Sacred Living, 365 Meditations and Celebrations
Dancing Up the Moon, A Woman's Guide to Creating
Traditions that Bring Sacredness to Daily Life
(both published by Conari Press)

Two Worlds One Light, A Memoir of a Medium

The Mother of Us All: Divine Mother Speaks - A Way Forward

and *Luminaria* a new poetry book ready for publication

Some endorsements for previous books:

Legendary Women Ancestor Series: Book One and Two and Three
The Legend of Randine, Entering the Sisterhood and
The Legend of Randine: The Laerdal Letters

I so enjoyed reading your new book, *Kisti's Royal Garden*. The stories, names and locations, felt so familiar to me.
Having grown up in the Midwest, my Lutheran Norwegian ancestors were pioneers in similar communities. You brought life to what seemed like my own family history.

Joy Cook
Daughters of Norway Grand Lodge President

Robin Lysne transports us to nineteenth century Norway in this beautifully written story of the spirited midwife Randine. I admired this atmospheric and carefully researched historical novel immensely.

Elizabeth McKenzie, author of *The Portable Veblen*, and *The Dog of the North*, Santa Cruz, CA Editor for Chicago Quarterly Review and Catamaran Literary Reader

My own Norwegian ancestry initially drew me to *The Legend of Randine*, and I was quickly engaged by the story of Randine. I highly recommend this beautifully written novel, not only for its compelling characters, but also for its previously untold drama of the development of midwifery in rural Norway.

Ruth Olsen Saxton, Professor Emerita of English, Mills College, Oakland, CA

Heart Path and Heart Path Handbook:

"Learning self-love is something everyone needs to learn. Heart Path offers readers a way to love themselves without limits."

John Gray, Ph.D. author of *Men are from Mars, Women are from Venus.*

Poems for the Lost Deer

"*Poems for the Lost Deer* is much more than poems. It is a tract that is, at once, lamentation and praise song, dirge and testament and manifestation. And an inquiry into values and hierarchy and a series of addresses to the faces of power. ... *Poems for the Lost Deer* invites readers to try to comprehend the scope and scale of the hillsides and of "what humans do."

C. S. Giscombe, author of Into & Out of Dislocation, and several other poetry books Professor at U.C. Berkeley, CA.

"*Poems for the Lost Deer* is passionate, compassionate, skillful, meticulous, graceful, vital, and heartbreaking..."

Heather Nagami, Editor of Overhere Press, Professor Northeastern University, Boston

This engaged and engaging sequence of poems by Robin Lysne sees permeable borders where others see boundaries; it is a kind of wordsmithery that is at once committed to changing our given worlds and to imagining spiritual worlds we have not yet reached.

Though the subject is ostensibly the historical destruction of the white deer at Pt. Reyes peninsula between 2007-8, the reach is broader. When a voice speaks from one of the poems to say: "We sing/our ghost/dance for/the fallen," deer and native and poet sing together of the past to question our future.

Through drawings, prose fragments, and lyrics, the poet deals in weighty matters, but with a deft touch that always allows the mysteries of nature to seep in and color everything. Let us listen hard to her singing.

David Allen Sullivan, Professor Cabrillo College, Author of Strong-Armed Angels, Every Seed of the Pomegranate.

Echoing Blake's Songs of Innocence and Experience, Robin Lysne's Poems for the Lost Deer documents the recent systematic slaughter of "non-native" Axis and Fallow deer from the Point Reyes National Seashore. Presenting "what happened" in an assemblage of overlapping voices -- factual "evidence". ..."Packing Slip Contents: / 20 dead assorted deer ñ minus racks"); and throughout it all the deer themselves -- first innocent ("Across this / field an apple tree / full of blossoms / run to it, sniff / stretching our necks / rub antlers on bark / scratch ears with hooves, / nuzzle young / we live / one more spring") then experienced ("Humans came / to stop the / hunters // They gave us / three more suns / before the massacre") and now forever gone ("thank you / for loving us / so well // We / forgive // Just know / love / is all / that / remains". This is a glimpse of the book Robin Lysne has given us, one whose time has come not a moment too soon.

Stephen Ratcliffe. Author of Real, Portraits and Repitition, and over 20 books of poetry and criticism, and was a long time Professor at Mills College.

Printed in the USA
CPSIA information can be obtained
at www.ICGtesting.com
CBHW080045010424
6154CB00001B/3